NORTH COUNTRY NOTEBOOK

George Vukelich

Introduction by Gaylord Nelson

North Country Press

Published 1987

NORTH COUNTRY PRESS
3934 Plymouth Circle
Madison, Wisconsin 53705

Illustrations by Daniel Metz
Designed by Thill Design, Inc.

First printing November 1987
Second printing January 1988

Printed in the United States of America

ISBN 0-944133-00-2 (cloth)
ISBN 0-944133-01-0 (paper)

*Some of these essays appeared originally in Wisconsin Trails; The
Capital Times; The Madison Press Connection and Isthmus of Madison.*

for Helen Louise
*whose campfires have brought Light to our journeys
and Warmth to our days*

Contents

Acknowledgments

I am particularly grateful to Betty Durbin for her skillful editing of this book and her unflagging enthusiasm that got us through every rapids along the way. We would have capsized without her and the other stalwart members of the Log Cabin Literary Society: Howard Mead, Jerry Minnich and Phill Thill who not only did all of the planning, but most of the paddling, to boot.

Appreciation for the use of excerpts from their books goes to: North Point Press for The Long-Legged House by Wendell Berry; Farrar, Straus & Giroux for The Survival of the Bark Canoe by John McPhee; Alfred A. Knopf for The Singing Wilderness, Open Horizons and Listening Point by Sigurd F. Olson; The University of Wisconsin Press for The Unpublished Journals of John Muir and John Muir: Son of The Wilderness by Linnie Marsh Wolfe; The MacMillan Company for North American Canoe Country by Calvin Rutstrum; The Stackpole Company for Stories of The Old Duck Hunters & Other Drivel by Gordon MacQuarrie; Harper and Row for Teaching A Stone To Talk by Annie Dillard; Atheneum for The Firmament of Time by Loren Eiseley; National Wildlife Federation for A Conservation Saga by Ernest F. Swift; Stanton and Lee for Walden West by August Derleth; The Stephen Greene Press for Animals Nobody Loves by Ronald Rood; St. Martin's Press for Trout Madness by Robert Traver; Voyageur Press for Journeys To Door County by Mike Link and Oxford University Press for A Sand County Almanac by Aldo Leopold.

Finally, a toast to Stuart Hanisch who believed in this book from the very first and that's why we saved him for the very last: *For good wine, for good food, for good friends, Thank God.*

Introduction

*H*ere is a book for everybody. It's a book for young folks, middle-aged, old folks and children, too. In that sense it is like *Alice In Wonderland* and *Through the Looking Glass*. Altogether, 79 delightful, funny, informative essays, vignettes, snippets of life, love, birds and many other things. It is, at once, profound and simple as most profound things turn out to be when someone like George Vukelich puts his pen to it.

This is a book about philosophy, people, places, turtles, crows, loons, owls and other creatures; it is about living, dreaming, fishing and just hiding out some place at the edge of a remote pond in the woods watching the trees grow and counting lily pads.

It's about animals, the human animal who somehow thinks he can safely flout the laws of nature and about all of the other animals who know better.

It's about bulldozers that work hard all week tearing up the countryside and then rest up over the weekend to start again on Monday.

It's about the stuff of Joseph Wood Krutch's depressing observation that—"If people destroy something replaceable made by humanity they are called vandals; if they destroy something irreplaceable made by God, they are called developers."

Vukelich writes of those things that commanded the talent and attention of Aldo Leopold, John Muir, Sigurd Olson, John McPhee and many others. Each of them said it eloquently and differently, but no one of them said it better nor any of them with as much wit and humor.

As you can see, George Vukelich talks about a lot of things. Most I haven't even mentioned, like Hugo Willie's Gasoline Emporium, concrete glaciers, mama mallards, wood boats, what the crow knows and Frank Lloyd Wright.

Edward Abbey in a recent book attributes to Confucius a humorous twist on an overused cliche (as contrasted with an under used one) which I am unable to verify as I am not on a first name basis with either Abbey or Confucius. In any event Abbey claims that Confucius said that "one word is worth a thousand pictures provided it's the right word." Well, Vukelich has a fine touch for choosing just the right word—indeed, lots of the right words.

Each of his little "stories" and perceptive slices of life are gripping, often hilarious, always entertaining, and, at the same time, teach a lesson without a lecture.

Gaylord Nelson
The Wilderness Society
Washington, D.C. 1987

North Country Notebook

SKY WALKER

Loon

*T*here was a time, Steady Eddy notes, when all the stuff you heard about the common loon was pretty derogatory. You never heard *"wise as a loon"* you heard *"crazy as a loon."* When folks said, "that's for the birds," they didn't mean eagles and ospreys, they meant cuckoos and loonies.

The cruelest judgment of all is that the silty, mucky bottoms of a million American lakes are never described as duckledroppings. It's always just plain old ordinary loonshit.

We are talking, Steady says, about a Rodney Dangerfield bird.

But of a sudden, our perception of the common loon has changed. It's not only getting respect, the loon is trendy. The loon is in.

The loon, Steady says, is a bird whose time has come.

The consensus is that since the release of the motion picture *On Golden Pond*, thousands, mayhap millions of people have simply fallen in love with this magnificent bird. And that's why the loon images are turning up on everything from T-shirts to tattoos.

You can't help thinking how pleased Sigurd Olson would be at this turn of events, for the common loon has been the symbol of the Sigurd Olson Environmental Institute at Northland College since its inception. In his book *Listening Point*, Sigurd told us:

> Above came a swift whisper of wings and as the loons saw us they called wildly in alarm, increased the speed of their flight, and took their laughing with them into the gathering dusk. Then came the answers we had been waiting for and the shore echoed and re-echoed until they seemed to throb with the music. This was the symbol of the lake country, the sound that more than any other typifies the rocks and waters and forests of the wilderness.

I identify with that because the loon has long been not just the logo, but indeed the totem of *North Country Notebook*, floating serenely as the Buddha up there for the past twenty years, diving only occasionally to check on how I was doing mucking around on the bottom.

Admittedly, other tribes have other totems in America today. We gather behind them as pilgrims behind the faces of God. It is indeed the retribalization of America. Some of us are Whales. Some of us are Ducks. Some of us are Trout— *Unlimited*. But most of us, as Steady first started observing at the old 400 Bar, are pretty obviously Loons.

Sigurd Olson wrote:

> Some say that loons eat too many fish and should be reduced in numbers, but as the population on most lakes is small, with usually only one or two per square mile of the area, this is a ridiculous assumption.

The loon is a symbol of the wild places. Like the whale and the wolf, it appeals mightily to the best part of us.

I don't know what scientist first called the loon "common." But as someone once observed in another context, it's a little like calling Jascha Heifetz a fiddler.

Two Loons

A young woman called the other morning to report that she had just been walking her dog down around the lake and had sighted two loons offshore, just fishing and hanging out.

She said that she was of two minds about them: ecstatic that they were there—"It's just like being up north to watch them" but concerned about their safety.

"I want them to stay," she agonized, "and I want them to go."

Even as she spoke, I thought of Aldo Leopold's observation that we humans can wear out the wild things, the wild places, by too much handling, too much fondling. We end up loving them to death.

"I also wanted you to see them," she said. Steady Eddy figures that's the kindest thing one human being has done for another since Frank Custer bought a round at the old 400 Bar.

She gave me directions and I was off, knowing full well that when you drop everything to go check out a couple of birds, most people put you down in the memory banks as a whole lot loonier than the birds you are checking out.

"Sometimes, when you've got your priorities on straight," Hugo Willie says, "people are apt to think you're a little skewed."

I saw the loon even before I got out of the car. By the time I walked down to the shore, the other one had surfaced fifty yards away. They looked to be loose and loafing, drifting and dreaming, but they were into serious fishing, working the bar like a pair of cat burglars, mindful of all the sleeping dogs in the neighborhood.

I don't know what seemed out of context—the loons in front of me or the roaring traffic behind me. Or me. Up north is the place for loons now. Once these southern lakes were their place. Indeed, lakes south of here and in Illinois were their place before humans destroyed the loons' habitat and the birds moved north.

They move through this old place on their migrations— "Nice place to visit," Steady says, "but you wouldn't want to

live here"—and like cross-country fliers, may be simply stopping over to take on fuel and let off tension.

The two loons were moving up the shore now, away from
the bar, working into deeper water, looking for fish, trolling.
I had never really thought about loons "trolling" until John
McPhee so described their fishing operation in *The Survival of
the Bark Canoe.*

> The loon is out there cruising still, in the spiraling
> morning mist, looking for fish, trolling.
>
> He trolls with his eyes. Water streams across his fore-
> head as he moves along, and he holds his eyes just below
> the surface, watching the interior of the lake. He is gone.
> He saw something and he is no doubt eating it now. When
> he dives, he just disappears. As a diver, there is nothing
> like him. Not even mergansers can dive like the loon. His
> wings close tight around his body, condensing every-
> thing—feathers, flesh—and he goes down like a powered
> stone, his big feet driving. He can go two hundred feet
> down. He can swim faster than most fish. What he catches
> he eats without delay. His bill is always empty when he
> returns to the surface and fifteen fish might be in his stom-
> ach. Because loons eat trout and young salmon, sportsmen
> (so-called) have been wont to shoot them—a mistaken act
> in any respect, because loons eat as well the natural ene-
> mies (suckers, for example) of salmon and trout.

Out on the lake, the two loons were silhouettes to the
naked eye now, moving away, gliding silently the way red-
tailed hawks do when they seem to coast into another dimension.

I wished that I had brought the field glasses, but then, if
I had brought them the loons wouldn't have been here. You
hang around with loons, Steady says, and you get to know their
moves.

Thousands of people were driving to work right past loons,
never seeing them, or, if seeing them, probably figuring they
were ducks or geese or whatever.

For a mini-second I wanted the loons to break their silence, because the traffic jam would back up to Bonnie Connie's. The loon's voice had caused panic, John McPhee wrote,

because it has been mistaken for the cry of a wolf. But it is far too ghostly for that:

It is detached from the earth. The Crees believed that it was the cry of a dead warrior forbidden entry to Heaven. The Chipewyans heard it as an augury of death. Whatever it may portend, it is the dominant sound in this country. Every time the loon cry comes, it sketches its own surroundings—a remote lake under stars so bright they whiten clouds, a horizon jagged with spruce.

The loon here is laughing again so I laugh back. He laughs. I laugh. He laughs. I laugh. He will keep it up until I am hoarse. He likes conversation. He talks this way with other loons. I am endeavoring to tell him that he is a hopeless degenerate killer of trout. He laughs.

Out on the lake, silent as hawks, the loons glide into another dimension.

What the Crows Know

I walked the oak woods the other day and something happened that has never happened before on any of the walks taken over a lifetime.

Without the sun, even at midday the air flowed around my face like ice water. The absence of light drained the life from the landscape, leaving that silvery grey cast that Sleepy Ed up in the Chain of Lakes Country always called "casket-colored." The snow creaked and crunched under the clubby shoe pacs.

I broke trail for a long time in the shadowless sea.

Lost in thought. Lost in time. Head down. Mindless perhaps. Not aware. Trudge. Drudge. Trudgery. Drudgery.

And then that familiar spooky feeling of being watched echoed through my brain case like a whisper through a darkened cavern.

I looked up.

There it was. A crow. Huge, perched above my head. Looking down at me. Absolutely motionless. Absolutely silent.

7

The sentinel crow, entrusted with the safety of the flock, discovered derelict. Caught off guard. Surprised.

But you don't surprise sentinel crows when you're dressed like a Christmas tree, struggling through the snowcrust like a thousand-pound moose.

No, I was witnessing something unusual. Something out of the ordinary. Something strange.

And even as the whisper in the cavern increased, suddenly other crows came flying to the sentinel's tree and to the trees around it.

They came by twos and threes and then they were dozens.

Gliding down softly as a snowfall.

Sitting as silently as stones.

All watching me.

The great carrion feeders, Nature's cleanup crews. "The undertakers," Sleepy Ed called them, and he was right.

I had seen these very crows all my life, in all seasons, summer and snow.

Then, suddenly they began to talk to each other and I knew they knew Something I was too dumb and sophisticated to learn.

After a while, they flew away as they had come. Unhurried. Silently. With a certain dignity. A certain nobility.

When they had gone and the sentinel tree stood empty, I sensed that I would see them again one day. Close above me. Close enough to touch.

And I will not be surprised.

Passenger Pigeons

I saw the passenger pigeon under the feeder again. I know the experts say the passenger pigeon is extinct, but they said the same thing about the coelacanth, that funny-looking fish that was supposed to have been dead and gone these millions of years, until one day it turned up in the nets of some South American fishermen and *bango!*

As Steady Eddy likes to put it when these unexpected shots happen: "There goes another good pitching theory rattling off the centerfield wall."

"We need to have our limits transgressed," Henry David Thoreau insisted, "and some life pasturing freely where we never wander."

It's not so strange to believe in passenger pigeons when you also believe in the Loch Ness monster, the yeti, and the woolly mammoth.

Not to mention, Steady adds, Bigfoot and Little Orphan Annie.

At a distance, the mourning dove could pass for the extinct passenger. And you can always pretend you don't see the mourning dove's trademark, that small spot of black-glossed-blue on the side of the head and upper neck beneath the ear.

The bird picks delicately at the strewn seeds on the ground, shy and spooky beneath the aggressive jays, ready to flee at any flash of movement, even a movement within the house.

Thoreau had it right when he observed that birds certainly are afraid of humans. They allow all other large creatures, excepting only one or two predators, to come near them, but not human beings. What does this fact signify?

Does it not signify, Henry answered himself, that we, too, are beasts of prey to them? Are we, then, true lords of creation, whose subjects are afraid of us, and with reason?

"They know very well," Henry sniffed, "that man is not humane as he pretends to be."

God, why couldn't the passenger pigeon have been as wary as the other birds?

Secretive as the ruffed grouse?

Sharp-eyed and suspicious as the red-tailed hawks?

Street-smart as crows working the golf courses?

According to the history books, the passenger pigeons darkened the Wisconsin skies in great clouds and broke the branches of trees when they roosted by the millions and just sat there, mild as milk, while men shot them, even clubbed them to death.

The passenger pigeon, Aldo Leopold said, was a biological storm.

It was the lightning that played between two opposing potentials of intolerable intensity: the fat of the land and the oxygen of the air. Yearly, the feathered tempest roared up, down, and across the continent, sucking up the fruits of forest

9

and prairie, burning them in a traveling blast of life. Like any other chain reaction, the pigeon could survive no diminution of its own furious intensity. When the pioneers subtracted from its numbers and destroyed much of its fuel, the pigeon's flame went out with hardly a sputter, or even a wisp of smoke.

"The wonder," Aldo wrote in amazement, "is not that the pigeon went out, but that it ever survived through all the millennia of pre-Babbittian time."

I watched the mourning dove, its head ever up for danger, like a hockey player burned forever by a searing blindside. Somehow it knows what happened here. We have taught this bird what its dead cousins never learned quickly enough.

We have taught this bird about us, about how deadly we are.

Our grandfathers, Aldo Leopold noted, were not as well-housed, fed, or clothed as we, and the efforts by which they bettered their lot are also those that deprived us of pigeons. Perhaps we now grieve because we are not sure in our hearts that we have gained by the exchange. The gadgets of industry bring us more comfort than the pigeons did, but do they add as much to the glory of the Spring?

Out there, in the February cold, the mourning dove is as silent as the snows, waiting for that season to return.

I don't really think that's the last passenger pigeon in the world. I think there's a pair of them, but they're cooling it.

Violence at the Bird Feeder

*T*here was another class in Nature 101 the other day. Right outside the picture window. Right below the bird feeder.

A bluejay killed a goldfinch.

It must have started when no human was watching.

Jo said she was upstairs and heard this terrible crying that sounded almost like a bleating, a whimpering, and when she came down to look, the bluejay was beating, enfolding the bleating goldfinch on the ground, an angel of death, violent

beyond belief, a flurry of anger. And then the bleating subsided, and the quiet that returned was the quiet of death.

I don't know why it seemed so terrible.

"Nature is the most natural thing in the world," Steady
Eddy likes to say, "and it ain't all dancing rabbits and cute little
mice with four fingers."

That bluejays are nasty-tempered comes as no surprise,
but that doesn't prepare you for the murderous attack, the
explosive assault that seems to come out of the blue without
rhyme or reason.

It's like the neighborhood grouch, of a sudden, snapping
and firing off a shotgun.

Maybe that's what seems so terrible.

We expect people to snap under the pressures of living.
When they do we can blame the economy or the marriage or
something. We creatures are supposed to be searching for "harmony." Nature's other creatures are supposed to be living in
it. *Living happily ever after.* Just like people. No, living more
wisely than people. Without fighting, without killing, without
eating each other up.

Walt Disney never prepared us for the real world on the
other side of the picture windows.

Every part of nature, Henry David Thoreau wrote in *Walden*, teaches that the passing away of one life is the making
room for another. Consider what a difference there is between
living and dying. To die is not to *begin* to die and *continue*; it
is not a state of continuance, but of transience. Nature presents
nothing in a state of death.

I don't know what the bluejay would have done had we
stayed inside and watched. We went outside to see what could
be done, or perhaps we simply went outside because we are
human and it is in our nature to witness the scenes of accidents
long after the sounds and screaming have subsided and there
is nothing at all that we can do.

The bluejay left.

Not in fear; not in retreat. It left without skulking.

The goldfinch was dead. It was not a baby, not a nestling.
God knows what happened to it, or rather, *why?*

Loren Eiseley, in his book *The Immense Journey*, described
the death of a baby bird as no one has ever described it.

11

"When I awoke," he writes in the chapter titled "The Judgment of the Birds," "dimly aware of some commotion and outcry in the clearing, the light was slanting down through the pines in such a way that the glade was lit like some vast cathedral. I could see the dust motes of wood pollen in the long shaft of light, and there on the extended branch sat an enormous raven with a red and squirming nestling in his beak."

The sound that awoke him, Eiseley reports, was the outraged cries of the nestling's parents, who flew helplessly in circles about the clearing. The sleek black monster was indifferent to them. He gulped, whetted his beak on the dead branch a moment and sat still. Up to that point the little tragedy had followed the usual pattern. But suddenly, out of all that area of woodland, a soft sound of complaint began to rise. Into that glade fluttered small birds of half a dozen varieties, drawn by the anguished outcries of the tiny parents.

No one dared attack the raven. But they cried there in some instinctive common misery, the bereaved and the unbereaved. The glade filled with their soft rustling and their cries. They fluttered as though to point their wings at the murderer. There was a dim intangible ethic he had violated, that they knew. He was a bird of death.

And he, the murderer, the black bird at the heart of life, sat on there, glistening in the common light, formidable, unmoving, unperturbed, untouchable.

The sighing died.

"It was then," Loren Eiseley declares, "I saw the judgment. It was the judgment of life against death. I will never see it again so forcefully presented. I will never hear it again in notes so tragically prolonged. For in the midst of protest, they forgot the violence."

There in the clearing, Eiseley marvels, the crystal note of a song sparrow lifted hesitantly in the hush. And finally, after painful fluttering, another took the song, and then another, the song passing from one bird to another, doubtfully at first, as though some evil thing were being slowly forgotten. Till suddenly they took heart and sang from many throats joyously together as birds are known to sing. They sang because life is sweet and sunlight beautiful. They sang under the brooding shadow of the raven. In simple truth, they had forgotten the raven, for they were singers of life and not of death.

"I knew I had seen a marvel," Loren Eiseley concludes, "and observed a judgment, but the mind which was my human endowment was sure to question it and to be at me day by day with its heresies until I grew to doubt the meaning of what I had seen. Eventually, darkness and subtleties would ring me round once more."

Again, the finches and the bluejays come, by turns, to our feeders. There has been harmony, or at least no further violence.

God knows what they are thinking.

Masters of Water and Sky

*I*t was a gray, misty morning when we put the boat in just off Willows Drive.

We couldn't see the far side of the lake and Mendota had that ocean-morning look early-bird fishermen know so well.

Mike, who watches the sky like a jet pilot, had checked with the Weather Bureau and while it sure looked like rain within the hour, the Weather Bureau had assured him there was no rain in the forecast.

"You just have to respect this water," Mike shrugs. "Always. Even when it's calm as a baby sleeping. The moment you lose your respect, you could damn well lose your life."

He cranked up the twenty-five-horse Merc and the tri-hull moved ahead slowly, skirting the weedbeds on tippy-toes. Once clear of them, we stepped up and planed out around Picnic Point, then swung west and drove smartly for Second Point and those world-famous perch.

Mike turned off the motor, stuck the transducer in the water, turned on the fish locater, and we drifted.

At twenty-six feet, the locator showed fish. Just off the bottom.

We anchored and fished. With big green hellgrammites. With little pieces of nightcrawler. And we caught perch. Dozens of them and they were all small. Many of them were deeply hooked and as these were thrown back and floundered on the still surface, the first herring gulls showed up around us.

We threw all the fish back as fast as we caught them and we moved. In eighteen feet of water, the fish were still small and we moved again. Into thirty feet. The same thing. Back shallow into fifteen feet. Hundreds of perch. All of them small. Hitting hard, many of them deeply hooked.

We kept throwing them back and the seagulls kept appearing as if from another dimension, suddenly and within a rod's reach. They simply materialized out of the mist like airplanes on Ground Control Approach, flying confidently down into a fog-shrouded landing.

We watched them, hovering over the injured, struggling small fish on the hushed surface.

The ghostly birds dipped and made passes, runs at the fish. Approaches. Glides. Flybys. And then, without landing, a gull would sooner or later be successful. Still airborne, the gull would snatch a perch up in its bill, struggle for altitude and swallow its catch while its flight-mates cried and called and scolded. Or were they cheering?

We watched the great gulls all morning. Feeding. Flying. Talking. The magical birds who watched over the waters of this world.

I had seen these very birds off the fantail of our troopship in the North Atlantic. I had seen them off our ore carrier in Lake Superior. As I saw them now, they filled me with awe and wonderment as always.

How, I asked Mike, finally, do the gulls know that something is dead or dying when they cannot possibly see it? Or hear it? Or smell it?

How? How?

We watched the seagulls without speaking. Masters of the sky above us. Masters of the waters below us.

As they called to each other, it seemed very clear and the most logical thing in the world, and we knew that they knew that we did not know.

Song of Longing and Home

W e spent the other night at a friend's farm near the Wisconsin River and as night poured into the bottomlands, the mournful cry of a whippoorwill filled the valley to its brim.

In the Wisconsin night, there is no voice—bird, beast or other—that sounds more isolated. More alone.

August Derleth, who used to live right around here, once wrote that perhaps it was because the whippoorwill song represented something unattainable, something in the dark, out of sight but never quite out of hearing. Something lonely. Desirable. Apart and lost. The whippoorwill, in a way, belonged to him, but it was not to be touched. Like childhood or youth. Perhaps that's what accounted for the nostalgia he read into that mystical birdsong. He once reminisced in *Walden West*:

> I know that psychiatrists tell us the urge to go home again, back to the irresponsible childhood, to the womb, might account for this kind of reaction, but to me it is a concept related not to the self nearly so much as to the desire of the self to be merged with the universe . . . not as in the psychiatrist's death wish . . . but in a spiritual oneness which is akin to the eternal quest to unity with God. . . .

When Augie was a child, he used to visit at the hilltop farm of his Aunt Annie Ring, west of Sac Prairie between Plain and Spring Green. For two or three weeks every summer he would stay at the farm with his cousins.

"The boy cousins," he recalled, "were either too young or too old to be companions. The girl cousins kept to themselves."

By the end of the first week, the novelty of the farm had worn off and he grew homesick for the Wisconsin River, its sloughs and its islands.

It was in those early-to-bed nights that he was awakened by the crying of whippoorwills, numerous in the darkness of the hills and valleys. Perhaps, somehow, the whippoorwills came

15

to represent the unattainable desire of that youthful heart, the longing for home, but home as more than a refuge for the body among familiar faces. Augie wrote later:

> I can understand how the whistling of a locomotive at night may sound lonely, how it may symbolize flight, escape; but I cannot say how the crying of a whippoorwill brings a tenuous mixture of joy and sadness out of the dark hills, nor how it represents all the lost hopes and dreams, how it stirs the visions and longing of boy and man as if it were not a bird, but the disembodied voice of night itself, of the very earth brooding in the darkness, the changed and the changeless, the living and the dead, time past and coming time, the boy who was, and the man who is, forever one. . . .

At my friend's farm, we listened to the loneliest voice in the Wisconsin night. When the voice finally stopped and was still, we lay on our backs, staring up at the silent Milky Way and listening for the voices of others.

I told my friend I heard nothing further.

My friend told me the same thing.

But the night was not lonely anymore.

Spooking Mama Mallard

*I*t was my fault in the first place.

As I walked the lake bank, all I saw were the two male mallards floating just a few feet offshore. I figured them for a couple of old bachelors who weren't raising families this spring and were just hanging out together, making small talk, snacking on a little daphnia, and not bothering anybody.

I even got an image of the Brenton boys, Charlie and Arthur, bathing in the warm shallows of their beloved Big Stone Lake, their faces and hands brown as berries, the rest of their bodies, covered for so many months by the longjohns, white as the bellies of walleyes.

It was when I moved closer that I saw the female.

She burst forth from the overhanging brush, and with her came a veritable fleet of little ones, bunched up, churning, a biomass of a dozen ducklings, swimming so tightly they touched, swimming so tightly you could mistake all the little mallards for another big mallard following Mama bumper to bumper.

I froze, knowing instantly that I had not only done something foolish, I had done something irresponsible.

Mama was spooked.

I don't know if it was panic. She wasn't close enough for me to see her eyes, but I just felt that those soft eyes would be wild.

She led her flotilla, at flank speed, past the two basking drakes, on line for the far shore, passing into deep water, open water, picking up speed—looking back at that safe haven that was no longer safe.

My God, she was taking them across the whole narrow bay.

I wanted to scream at her to stop. I wanted to scream at the drakes to stop her. I wanted to scream at *Something* to stop her.

I wanted to scream because of the guilt I felt.

In the end, I said a prayer for all of us.

In my mind's eye, the biggest, hungriest, northern pike in the whole lake had picked up the sudden surface movements and was now homing in on the brood, rising, rushing, about to slash. . . .

They wouldn't be out there if only I had been aware.

They were out there needlessly.

Needless. Heedless.

When I was a toddler with Baba Jula and Tata they said I squeezed the life out of a baby chick before either of those solicitous grandparents could do anything. I don't remember that at all. But if a duckling dies on this trip, I'll remember who squeezed the life out of it.

Some people would observe that it's anthropomorphism to feel that way about a mallard hen or a mallard duckling, or any life that isn't human. But not Henry David Thoreau.

"It would be worth the while to ask ourselves," he wrote in *Walden*, "is our life innocent enough? Do we live *inhu-*

manely, toward man or beast, in thought or act? To be serene and successful we must be at one with the universe. *The least conscious and needless injury inflicted on any creature is to its extent a suicide."*

Out in the middle of the open water, the fast-traveling swimmers were streaking along without incident. They were featureless now, too far away to have faces or flesh, they were dark silhouettes fleeing, simply fleeing. I watched with a fascination, a fixation. I watched for death to come.

Once, when The Old Man and I were anchored for walleyes on Big Stone, a loon drifted in, diving, fishing quietly, and then it began yelling and making a racket I hadn't heard ever before and haven't heard since. It was struggling, wings beating, screaming, as anchored in one spot as we were. We finally went over and saw up close. A big musky had it by the leg, but the bird was too big and strong to drown. Maybe if we hadn't gone over. . . . A duckling hit by a pike would simply disappear.

On the far side of the narrow bay, wild, brushy, near-inaccessible, the mallard hen and her ducklings had slowed down, coasted, stopped. Even squinting you couldn't see them clearly, but they looked to be poking around, intact. Without a care in this world.

Send Me a Hawk

I took the blue canoe and fished the marsh Sunday morning. I went alone but I met a couple of old friends out there on the mudflats. Augie Derleth and The Old Man. Well, Augie, for sure. The Old Man was there all right, but he never really showed his hand.

First, I didn't fish at all. Just paddled and poked into all the secret places of the marsh. The chambered potholes where the mallards were paired out of everybody's sight but God's. The ancient sunning logs on which the turtles lay absorbing heat and never really sleeping. The scoured whitish circles on the shallow bottom where the bluegills would nest and spawn.

I put down my paddle and took up my rod.

Send me a fish, I asked The Old Man.

The sun was warm on my back. The breeze, cool on my face. I felt like the turtles on their log. Was Somebody watching me the way I watched them? I looked up into the sky. Blue. Endless. Empty. Send me a hawk, I asked August Derleth. A red tail.

Why does the hawk remind me of Augie? Was it because he loved the hawk? Was it because he lived like a hawk? Augie wrote in *Walden West*:

What is it about hawks that strikes the note of kinship with which I am always moved at the sight of them—a feeling amounting almost to the conviction of sharing the hawk's solitude as well as its ecstasy in flight, which enables me to float aloft while I am prone upon a hilltop, watching that magnificent bird ride the air current invisible to any human eye, high up, remote in heaven? Surely the hawk is master of all it sees—as much king of this domain as its majesty implies.

It soars, it floats, it circles, turns, vaults, dives—it makes all sky and cloud, wind and air, all earth its own. The hawk which thus for these hours belongs to me, also claims me for its own without more than a cursory awareness of my existence. The keen, discerning eye takes in heaven and earth, scans ground and water, knows the inhabitants of that upper air—ospreys and swallows, all others are below its range.

Its scream drifts down the buttes of heaven, its shadow crosses slope, plain, river, village, so small a cross of darkness on the land, so small a mark of darkness in the sky where it goes by with a rare beauty that has within it all the lost beauty of the wilderness that was America.

And suddenly there was a hawk, wings set, wheeling above the marsh. A red tail. It circled for a full minute, then it dropped like a stone into the horizon.

"Thank you, Augie," I said. Out loud.

I never got a fish. One small bump and gone. That could have been anything.

Later, with the canoe on top of the wagon and all the gear inside, I took one long, last look at the eternal marsh. I could almost hear The Old Man saying: *You wanted a fish. You wanted a hawk. You did fifty per cent this morning and a lot of people didn't do fifty percent. And they went to church.*

You son-of-a-gun, I told The Old Man. Out loud.

Canada Goose

As I approached, the Canada goose got to its feet, the neck rising like a cobra, poised to strike, the body built to swim the upper air, waiting, waiting.

I gave the bird a wide berth. I even told it out loud that there was nothing to fear from me. Not hurt. Not harm. *Not to worry.*

The bird watched. And listened. And then it struggled down to the water, swaying from side to side, looking unbalanced, unsynchronized.

It's the condition that Steady Eddy likes to describe as "coming untorqued," wherein the front end and the back end don't have it together anymore. Steady's description is usually applied to people in the late evenings, but today it applied to this uncoordinated goose in the midafternoon.

The goose fell, rather than flowed, into the water, and there, at land's end, it stretched itself magnificently with one strong, beating wing. The right one. The left wing clung to the body, immobile, bent grotesquely. Broken.

The goose propelled itself out into deeper water, looking back all the while. Wary. I felt as though I had crippled that goose, brought it down out of the skies, and was responsible for the death that would come to it on the ground.

I put the field glasses on it, and as it leaped into sharp enlargement I knew instinctively that those high-resolution eyes out there on the water saw me better, knew me better, than I, with the coated Japanese lenses, would ever see the goose.

It bothered me that the bird was hurt. It bothered me even more that the bird sought no help. It was a judgment.

20

"It's tough to fool an old bird," Steady says, "That's how they come to get old."

The goose, the lame-duck goose, floating out there beyond the reach of man, now set its course for the far shore and made headway unevenly, like a skiff with mismatched oars. It was working mightily, and yet its movement slipped and skewed. Its zigzag wake told all who saw that the swimmer was no longer whole, no longer as formidable as before, no longer able to fly the skies. Now it was destined to meet death when next these marshlands froze.

"Nature," Steady shrugs. "It ain't all dancing ducks and talking mice with four fingers."

It's funny how easily you can empathize with a Canada goose in a way you never could with a fish or a dragonfly or a worm.

Perhaps it's because we don't regard the goose as alien. It has long been our conceit that Canada geese were something like people. They loved their freedom. They were as gregarious as Shriners. And they mated for life.

Mel Ellis of the *Milwaukee Journal* and Little Lakes told me once about the terrible trouble he got into with a national outdoors magazine on which he served as contributing editor over a goose story he had written. The editors said he was identifying too much with the geese, being "too anthropomorphic." *An-thro-po-mor-phic*, Mel had pronounced it, slowly, as though it was some exotic disease you had come down with and the doctor wanted to be sure you knew it was exotic. And fatal. Then, because Mel would not change his mind about being anthropomorphic, the magazine changed its mind about Mel being contributing editor.

You start empathizing with critters, and it becomes harder to kill them. You start giving the chickens names, and you could wind up a vegetarian.

Thoreau writes in *Walden* that he came upon a small painted turtle on its back, its head stretched out as if to turn over, and when he stopped to investigate, the turtle drew in its head at once in the shell that "was partially empty." He reports that he could see through the shell from side to side, the entrails having been extracted through large openings just in front of the hind legs. The dead leaves were flattened where the turtle had been operated on, and were a little bloody. Most likely, he speculates, it was done by some bird of the heron kind with a long and powerful bill.

"Such is Nature," Henry David concludes, "who gave one creature a taste or yearning for another's entrails. . . ."

It's not easy to identify with that bird.

It's even harder, says Steady, to identify with that turtle. The goose is easier.

And yet, the same spirit that is in me is not only in you—it is in the Canada goose as well. It is in other birds. It is in turtles. It is indeed in the very stones that we are pleased to say have no life, have no spirit.

Anyone who has stood for long in the shadows of the great mountains would say that only softly. And then would not say that at all.

The goose disappeared into the far marsh, and I went to watch the black bass spawn.

WAITING FOR THE FISH TO FIND YOU

Waiting for Cats

"**Y**ou can take your *walleye* fishing," Steady Eddy was saying, "and your *bass* fishing. And your *musky* fishing. . . ."

He paused, giving me time to contemplate where I could take them.

"*This*," he declared, lobbing out the huge chunk-bait the way Dynie used to fungo flyballs, "is fishing."

We were sitting on the Flats in Lake Mendota's North Bay with four poles between us, soaking for catfish. The Flats winding into Westport are murky. Shallow. Riverine. Cattails stand knee-deep in the marsh. Red-winged blackbirds gabble incessantly in that lush jungle. The place has the look and smell of the primal. Ooze and muck, and prehistoric beginnings. Without closing your eyes you are on the Wisconsin, or the Mississippi, or any of the world's backwaters, away from the main currents, away from the deep channels, just sitting in the sloughs and staring at the huge bobbers that look like Japanese ocean fishing floats.

Steady arranged himself in the stern, got out a cigaret, settled back against the Merc and stared out at the huge bobbers.

"This also," he observed, "beats working."

It seems like the easiest fishing in the world.

All you need is a stout rod, even stouter bait. Cast out the bait, put the rod down, then wait. And it's precisely the *waiting* that makes catfishing—still-fishing—the hardest fishing of all.

You don't need a lot of technique or sophisticated electronics or expensive gear. All you need is *patience.* That's what makes it so hard.

Only people don't say: "It's so hard." They say it's boring or it's not exciting or it's stinky. They say that if they wanted to do it, they could do it; *anybody* could do it because it's so damn simple.

But it's not so simple.

"All this water," Steady says, going right to the heart of the problem, "and the fish have to come to *you."*

As usual, Steady has got the thing—hook, line and sinker.

In the company of The Old Man or Dynie Mansfield, you could always go and find the walleyes. In the company of Bob Resch, you could always go and find the muskies. In the company of Reinfeldt and Zimmerman, you could always go and find the trout.

But in the company of Steady Eddy, you just sit on the Flats and wait for the fish to find you.

That's why you think of the Wisconsin and the Mississippi and River Congo and River Nile and River Amazon. This is the way it began. Humanoids crouched, poised, waiting in the shallows. Waiting.

Steady Eddy looked at me the way pitchers do when they just *know* what's on the batter's mind.

"Dick Stenlund," Steady said. "Stenlund had the patience for catfishing."

You think of all the hours Stenlund spent just waiting for catfish; it's no wonder he hit one that went twenty-two pounds.

You think of all the years Stenlund spent just waiting for his pitch; it's no wonder he hit softball fast-pitchers like he owned them.

Patience, sayeth The Lord.

Not to mention Steady Eddy, Catfish Stenlund, Dynie, and every mortal who has gone to find fish and realized finally that it is the fish that find you.

Only one fish finds us—Steady's five-pound channel cat.

Out in the big lake, police divers are trying to find a drowned man.

An Old Time Warden

We were off for our daylong float down the Lemonweir River, putting in at Mauston below the dam, and with luck surviving to our take-out point at Cliff House on the Wisconsin.

The river has a Southern feel to it—the water coffee-colored, the current undulating with dark mysteries. On the banks, rows of forked branches marked the beats of the patient people who set their stout poles here and wait for the catfish to feed.

Only one fisherman waited for them this morning.

He had the look of the river professional, gear strong enough to derrick out a four-ply tire, wearing an almost-smile as he took in the ridiculous ultra-light in my hands.

He was up from Illinois, he said, to fish for cats.

He came up often and he fished right here, in the pool below the dam, because it was usually good, but not right now.

We wished him Luck and drifted around the first bend.

"Can you believe that," Perce said. "All the way up from Illinois to catfish?"

There were probably a thousand places closer to home, and the man from Illinois probably knew that as well as anybody, but that was the trouble: *They were closer to home.*

Maybe he came here because he liked the name of the river: *Lemonweir*. Or the comforting mystery of that pool below the dam. Or the fact that he could fish from the bank on a Sunday morning and be absolutely alone, which is not always possible in those thousand other better places.

"It is pleasant," Henry David Thoreau wrote in *The River*, "to remember those quiet Sabbath mornings by remote stag-

27

nant rivers and ponds, when pure white water-lilies, just expanded, not yet invested by insects, float on the waveless water and perfume the atmosphere. Nature never appears more serene and innocent and fragrant."

We drifted and cast for smallmouths, and went down around another bend.

We should have been getting farther and farther from any road, yet there, right beyond the high bank, was a pickup truck crashing through the brush like a moose.

It caught up with us, passed us, and stopped at the next bend. The driver walked down to the sandspit and waited for us.

He wore a black hat and a black shirt and a little badge. He was also carrying a weapon, holstered, on his hip. I thought it was a 4.2 mortar, but Perce said later it was probably only a Magnum. The kind that will penetrate not only you, but your engine block to boot.

He said he was a warden, walked out on the sand to the point that his boots were getting wet, and showed his identification.

"Here's mine," he said affably. "May I see yours?"

We beached the canoe and I handed over my fishing license. He thanked me and passed it back.

Perce, in the stern, was going through his wallet.

His wallet takes some going through, because Perce keeps everything in there that ever happened to him, including his discharge from the Navy, gasoline ration cards from World War II—"the Big One," Steady says—and hunting and fishing licenses from the Year 1.

But, unfortunately, not for the Year 1981.

The closest he could come was 1974. He had *two* fishing licenses for 1974, his and Barb's.

Close, you see the warden thinking. *Close, but no cigar.*

"It's in my other pants," Perce said.

That must have impressed the warden. Or maybe Perce's honest blue eyes.

"I'm going to validate your license for *today*." the warden said, writing on it, "and when you get home, you send me the number of your '81 license."

"It's a Sportsman's," Perce said.

"Good," the warden said.

"A warden with common sense," Perce said in admiration. "Makes you feel a whole lot better about the DNR."

It reminded me of what Ernie Swift, in his book *A Conservation Saga*, had said about the old-time wardens:

> They traveled in pairs, carried sidearms, and were careful not to cross in front of a light after dark. . . . To survive and maintain any standing with local contemporaries and critics, they had to be rugged realists, shrewd improvisors with real outdoor talents and a liking for campfires. They had to be able to line out a pack string or pole a boat upstream in white water; they had to be better than average with an axe, with firearms and a compass. . . . They had to turn to and pack in fish fingerlings, trap beaver on complaint, run compass, give a fair estimate on a timber stand, trail a wolf or track a man. They used ain't and scrupulously avoided any scientific jargon and could drink from a jug by using an index finger and an elbow. They also had philosophies tempered in the crucible of wind, water, prairie and trees. They left some mighty big tracks.

It was the first time a warden had *ever checked* Perce. Perce kind of liked that. It was like Ernie Swift said.

Algoma

We three came to spend the weekend fishing for chinooks off the coast of "the trout and salmon fishing capital of Wisconsin," Algoma.

We three being Guy Lewis, the pipe-smoking, endlessly patient electronics wizard who also functions as copy chief for *The Capital Times*; Guy's Fitchburg friend and neighbor, Tom Helmer, master of the Starcraft *Marrilee* who in real life manages the Madison office of the A.B. Dick Company; and yours truly, a bottlewasher of some little reputation.

We came to crew the *Marrilee* and to catch salmon under the watchful guidance of its able and expert skipper, who trolls these waters every weekend, from ice-out to freeze-up, and who has been doing it for seven fish-filled years.

Helmer's route, week after week, is a groove.

He takes 151 out of Madison, past Columbus, Beaver Dam, Fond du Lac, and the southeast shore of Lake Winnebago and it's light traffic, soft travelin' all the way and there is that expectancy, that unlimited-open-horizon-kind-of-expectancy, that rushes over you when you first notice that somehow, the countryside seems to have opened up and now you can see for miles. The sky just seems higher, wider. The air is transparent. The colors radiant. The very road sign glows with an aura: *151 North.*

But, for me, the real turn-on comes when we reach Manitowoc and swing north on 42. To the right lies the brooding, great inland sea. Ahead lie Two Rivers. Point Beach. And a part of my boyhood. Maybe the best part.

This was in the Old Days. This was before they put coho into the lake. Or chinooks. Or nylon nets. This was in the days when the LeClair tug took a ton of laketrout in a morning's lift and I got to steer on the run back south to Two Rivers.

The herring gulls were waiting even as Germain and his brothers moored to the spiles and began to crank up the heavy, creosoted potnet. As the net came slowly, painfully up from the depths, it formed a floor under the fish, forcing them to the surface where they broke into view, splashing and thrashing in a frenzy of beating whitewater. The brothers shovelled them out with long-handled shallow scoopnets and dumped them into the open hold of the tug.

The gulls were everywhere. Clouds of them crying and screaming and wheeling above the fishgrounds, soaring and sailing in loose, easy circles over the furious work below. Others floated beyond the perimeter of the spiles, serene and silent in the rolling green water. And still others sat the very spile tops, closer, braver than the rest, waiting for the fishing to be finished and the cleaning to begin.

After all the nets had been lifted and emptied and set once more, the brothers would often take off their slickers if the late morning was still and the sun was strong. Germain would put a cigaret in his mouth and never touch it again while they sharpened their shortbladed knives and started in to clean the catch.

One quick slice from the anal fin up to the head. Razor strokes around the gill rakers and the powerful, hand stripping pull that tore the guts out of the fish, leaving the inner satiny lining, bloodstreaked and barren, the emptied fish fresh and dead and lofted into the boxes, to be iced and packed for shore.

They threw the fish offal into fifty-five-gallon oildrums and sold it to farmers who had pigs, but the gulls followed all the way back as if the stink on the wind was enough to sustain them while they waited for parts of fish to be flung into the wake.

As the brothers gilled and gutted and talked happily in the sunlight, sometimes dozens, sometimes hundreds of lives were being snuffed out, disembowelled, ended.

The cold otherworldly bodies of the great laketrout beating against each other, helpless against each other, helpless in an alien environment.

Schooled for the last time on this good earth. Swimming for the first time in an ocean of air. Some surviving to the very moment of the knife. None surviving beyond.

I felt sorry for the fish but I never told Germain or any of the LeClairs that because they were commercial fishermen and professional and this was a way of life with them all and a job. I also thought they would laugh at me.

I felt sorry for the gulls in a way, too. They were scavengers, eating garbage, eating offal.

It was only later that I discovered of a sudden that we have much in common with fish who beat their lives away in an alien environment and with herring gulls who search through the world's garbage.

It was only later that I discovered we were really all like the LeClair family on the fishtug Ione.

An iron hull and the hand of God holding us. This is the way we must go.

Germain and his brothers are all gone now. Some buried. Some scattered. All blown away. I sense today that they knew what was in my mind about the fish and the gulls all along. I sense that because I am older now than Germain was then.

And as sure as the brooding great inland sea still rolls under God's waiting gulls, I know now that no LeClair would have laughed at that little boy after all.

Turtle

We had just come off the Flats with two fair-sized catfish and were carrying the gear up to the car where Dyna-Ann waited.

Steady Eddy had called her to come get us because the big lake was still boiling with white caps and the trip home in the little boat would have been a white-knuckler.

All day long we had bounced around like a cork in the rolling waters of North Bay and watched the rich blueblooded sloops parade down the channel like leashed greyhounds straining to chase rabbits.

We stood at the car trunk. Sunburnt. Windblown. Beaten.

It was hard to tell what Dyna-Ann's eyes were doing behind the sunglasses.

"Never a dull moment," she said, "with Steady Eddy."

A couple of fisherpersons came over to get a closer look at the catfish. After all, one weighed eight pounds, the other a little over thirteen.

One of the men standing there had that tanned, neatly groomed small-town look that always makes me think of forest rangers and the Highway Patrol. Crisp. The name patch over his shirt pocket said "John."

"Nice fish," he said. "One about thirteen?"

Steady went to open the trunk and Dyna-Ann leaned out of the window.

"Don't forget about Oscar," she warned. "He's still in there."

Steady opened the trunk. And there was Oscar. The near-thirty pound snapping turtle that Stenlund and Parisi had caught and given Steady to clean. Steady lifted the turtle by the tail and set it down on the asphalt.

John stuck his boot toe down and the snake-head struck, the jaws clinging to the leather.

The little knot of fisherpersons oohed appropriately. "Geez," somebody said.

"Whattaya take for it?" John asked Steady.

"It ain't for sale," Steady told John.

John stared at the turtle for a long time and then at Steady.

"My father used to be a turtle hunter," he said. "I figure this one's pretty old. I figure about fifty years."

"That's what I figured," Steady said.

The turtle sat immobile as some great weathered stone. It had a dark, greenish, yellowish cast. There was an aura, an ambience of moss, of age, of alien mudbanks and river bottoms. It was something primal, something powerful. And at this age no longer had any natural enemies in the water. Except one.

"My son and I," John said, "came across one about this size and I was ready to kill it. He asked me if I realized how old that turtle was. I did. And that turned me around on killing. My son turned me around on killing. If you sell me this one, I'll put it back in the river."

John and Steady looked at each other and then at the turtle.

"I've killed a lot of turtles," Steady said. "I was having trouble bringing myself to kill this one."

John nodded, kind of smiled, and plucked the turtle up by the tail. The little knot of witnesses followed them down to the water's edge.

"I must be getting old," Steady sighed. "And that wasn't even my turtle."

Dyna-Ann and I looked at each other and I felt we were thinking the exact same thing. We were thinking *that turtle was everybody's turtle*.

What she said out loud was: "Never a dull moment with Steady Eddy."

Fishing Alone

I don't know what possessed me, but something possessed me the other day and I had to go stand hip-deep in a trout stream.

Maybe it was the months of sitting on hardwater that had chilled my chemistry until it cried for sun-warmed meadowlands. Maybe it was the passing of Ivan Nestingen and Don Anderson and Jimmy Demetral only days apart.

33

Maybe it was, as The Old Man always used to insist, only the sap loosening up after a hard winter and beginning to flow between my ears again.

As I headed the wagon west, I told myself that what I was really doing was going to "field-test" the new hip boots that Scott Wirth had sold me to replace the old ones slashed into garterbelt lengths on a barbed-wire fence along this very creek on the Last Day of last season.

Of course, that wasn't the real reason I was going.

Scott Wirth's hip boots would be as leak-proof and watertight as his word and the whole world knew that so I wasn't going to field-test the boots at all.

I was going to field-test something else.

An hour west of Madison, I drove into that other World.

The wagon dipped down into the beloved valley and the Great Magical Kingdom spread to the horizon. The grasses lay bright green, newborn, ancient as Earth herself, and yet innocent as baby's hair.

The sacred grove of the oak opening, barely in bud, stretched its arms, like the gnarled limbs of Old People to the God of warmth and Life.

The river lay curled, serene as a string, like a snake sunning itself.

I put on the hip boots, left the wagon and climbed the fence stile. It came to me then that I was the only living human being in this valley this midmorning and I knew why I had come here.

I moved along the tender grasses, among the old ghosts, a kind of time traveler, moving between the frozen, fixed Past and the flowing, bubbling Present.

I crossed the creek a dozen times, a crazy otter kind of trail. I skipped and splashed and yelled down the valley a hooray and thank you, God. I stood hip-deep—well, just below the boot-tops—in the best hole on the whole river and let the laughing, chuckling rapids speak of Delbert and Zeke and Ed and the Thursday Trouting and Squirreltail Social Club who hold church here regularly.

In the curved bank of the oxbow, cliff swallows worked on their new sublets. At the tail of the pool, a trout rose quietly. Then another.

Beyond this place, the reaches of the upper river lay still as a painting, the Elysian Fields stretching to the mystical horizon, waiting for Something, What Thing I know not. But Expectant. Waiting. I almost expected to see The Old Man.

Next time, I may bring the flyrod. Then again, maybe not.

Opening Day Rituals

One of the benefits of hanging out at the bait shop is that sooner or later you get to meet all the Old Timers in town.

"Since the 100 Bar closed," Steady Eddy says, "this is pretty much it."

Steady jests.

While it is true that the free beer dispensed here on the Opening Day of the fishing season has become a tradition of sorts (the opening of the *Fasching* season, some of the younger anglers call it) it is equally true that many of the venerated Old Timers no longer drink or, for that matter, dissipate their energies in any fruitless, bootless pursuit—*fishing* being the sole exception.

They come to the bait shop like the Roshi comes to the Zendo.

"The Roshi," Gary Snyder reports in *Earth Household*, "tells these poor souls beating their brains out night after night that 'the Perfect Way is without difficulty' and he means it and they know he's right."

We were sitting around the bait shop the other day, just sort of hanging out with the minnow tank, when in walked the Roshi. The Perfect Teacher. The Old Timer.

Steady says you can always tell by the minnow buckets they carry. Nothing plastic. Or Styrofoam. Or itsy-bitsy-cutesy, like a yogurt carton.

"They carry old pails," Steady says, "from the old school. Big. And built. Your basic Heavy Metal."

The Old Timer wanted suckers.

"If you got them six or eight inches long," he specified. "Two dozen."

Steady has them. Steady has baitfish big enough to filet and fry. Big bait, big northerns.

It turns out that the Old Timer is a northern pike fisherman from way back. He started out fishing them with a hand-line, and that's what he fishes them with today. A hand-line. No pole, you understand. Just the sucker on one end and the Old Timer on the other without anything in between. You twirl the sucker around your head and then throw it out into the water and let it soak.

"Like a cowboy throwin' a lasso," Steady says. "A sober cowboy."

The Old Timer says it's still the most effective way to fish northern pike.

"Nothin' fancy," he admits. "But I've taken northerns out of Lake Mendota that way for years. Big northerns, I've taken a lot of 20-pounders and over. A lot."

He said that about twenty years ago or so, the state had a test net in Mendota and they came up with a northern that weighed over forty pounds. He said the late Al Koppenhaver, the game warden, told him and swore it was true.

"They put that one back and nobody caught it," the Old Timer said. "Leastwise, nobody ever reported catching it. I know for a fact there's other big northerns out there nobody is catching."

He said he harnessed the suckers and he fished them live and he fished them dead. When they died, he just froze them individually and used them until he ran out.

Harnessing the suckers led me to think of The Old Man, who always had one soaking for muskies whenever he finally located the walleyes and we were going to be anchored in one spot for a spell. The walleyes came in to feed on the minnows. And muskies came in to feed on everybody. The Old Man conducted some pretty heavy lessons out on those northern rock-bars. Doc Hasler at the Limnology Lab would have been proud.

It is this knowledge of what's going on below the surface waters that leads one to agree eventually with the Renaissance fishing-man, Sven Berlin; who captured as well as anyone the fright of the terrible discovery.

Fishing, therefore, Sven Berlin observed, is not only a matter of meditation, of peaceful moments in which the reflected images are as real as those above the water, through which fish move and thought is seen upon the fin, turning, nuzzling the mud, searching with its golden eye for a pearl. It is also a dream of prehistory.

"We touch fintips with the coelacanth," Sven writes, "with the coelacanth who may well have emerged from the sea to negotiate with the problems on land. It is the great ocean behind life from which all things emerge and to which all must return."

The Old Timer left with his heavy pail and his light dignity, moving like a monk about the quiet cloister, deceptively young, deceptively old. The Shangri-la syndrome—like staring at Frank Lloyd Wright's Taliesen until you swear it was built yesterday, until you swear it was built a thousand years ago.

We talked about that dignity, that *quality*, and Steady got very serious.

"You know," he said. "The Old Timers have that *something*. This one catches fish with a hand line. Charlie Bran used to catch fish with just a canepole. One canepole and he would outfish *everybody*."

Bill Best puts it another way.

"It's not the gear," he says, pointing to his head, "it's what's up here."

"Not too long before Charlie died," Steady said, "he came in for minnows and I insulted him. I didn't mean to, but I did. I just figured that at his age and all the fun he had fishing, I just figured I wouldn't charge him for the minnows."

He shook his head, reliving that moment.

"Charlie," Steady recalled, *"didn't want free minnows*; he didn't expect free minnows, and he paid for them, *cash*."

Charlie Bran. Al Koppenhaver. The Old Timers. *Memento mori.*

The Last of the Canepole Fishermen

I was catching biggie bluegills in University Bay the other day and dreaming about the cabin up at Eagle River when it filled my head like a mantra or a sinus condition that I must be among the Last of the Canepole Fishermen in all of Vilas County.

Now it must be understood that I am not a true canepole fisherman because I do not fish exclusively with a canepole.

I have fishing poles for different kinds of fishing.

Musky rods. Salmon rods. Steelhead rods. Bass rods.

Some are spinning rods and some are casting rods and they are all part of quote Systems end quote that are designed to take specific fish in specific ways.

I have flyrods for trout and flyrods for bass and flyrods for panfish. I have heavy duty rods for channel catfish and light action jigging sticks for winter bluegills.

And I have two canepoles.

They aren't really the Old-Fashioned ones from the Ancient Times. Those were one-piece jobs, long as a city block, and when The Old Man carried a bundle of them atop his 1932 Buick—the Al Capone model—he always tied on red bandanas fore and aft to warn traffic of the extra-long load.

The Old Man fished Everything with those canepoles. And he caught Everything.

Walleyes out of Arbor Vitae. Smallmouth bass out of the Three Lakes Chain. Panfish out of Everywhere. I remember the time he caught a monstrous dogfish out of Tichigan. And an even bigger garfish out of Pewaukee.

The Old Man had canepoles all his life and he used them even after he got the money and moved up to the Pflueger Supreme reels and later, the Fenwick fancy rods. He always kept a bunch of the canepoles on a rack outside the garage wall. Hooks, lines, and sinkers. Real corks too. Fully rigged and ready to go when you were. Nobody used them much in his last years and now they're gone even as he is gone and the garage wall has a new coat of paint and a neat flower box.

My canepoles are three-piece affairs, the sections screw into each other and they are made by Lew's Poles in Alabama.

I like the way they look, jointed together, fully rigged, now varnished dark, shiny. They're simple. They're efficient. They're beautiful.

As beautiful, I think, as any fishing pole I own and I don't exclude the sacred bamboo flyrods.

I don't use the canepole very often.

Just up at the Cabin. And just on blindingly sunny days.

Then, in the lazy midmorning, wearing only the old swim trunks, I take one canepole, a can of worms, a five-gallon pail and go fish bluegills from the canoe.

Like the little kid that I once was. And still am.

When I catch fifty bluegills and the pail is sloshing full, I stop. It doesn't usually take too long to take the fifty.

Just long enough to see, if you really look for it, a 1932 Buick, parked back in the pines and a glimpse of red bandanas fluttering through the branches.

Fishing for the Silence

*T*he whole family was packing for the trip to the North Country cabin again, and after all the years we've been doing this, I finally realized something I never realized before.

We are taking fewer fish poles along.

Granted, we are also taking fewer kids along—fewer of everything, in fact, because these days we scoot up there in the little Honda instead of the Big Old Wagon, and climbing into that peewee cockpit makes you feel like all those oldtimey *kamikaze* pilots who used to get zippered in there without their parachutes and credit cards.

But not too many years ago, we'd go north with so much fishing tackle we looked like Wes Zulty Sports on wheels. Those weren't exactly my formative years, but I was under the spell of Dynie Mansfield, who walked the quarterdeck like Captain Hook, and whose basic preachment about provisions was simple: *If one is good, then two is better.*

My truly formative years were spent with The Old Man, who always tied bundles of enormous canepoles on top of the Al Capone Buick, replete with running boards and baggage racks, and we'd set sail for the North like some Chinese junk coasting along in the tea trade.

We took all the fishing tackle we owned, because we went Up North to go *fishing*, and in those Depression days, you fished for the whole clan left back in South Milwaukee. We fished for

39

food as much as we fished for sport, and we were as serious about it as any tuna boat out of San Pedro.

I remember The Old Man crating up limits of walleyes in ice and sawdust and sending the wooden boxes south on the trains out of Minocqua, Eagle River, and points north. I also remember him burying so many fish in John Weiss' icehouse on Island Lake that we never found half of them, and, John said, they kept turning up so long after the season closed that people thought they were poached.

Nowadays, we take a couple of flyrods, a couple of ultra lights, and that's it for tackle.

We fish every day at the cabin and we eat fish every day, but I don't think we go up there just to fish.

And come to think of it, I don't think we ever did.

I recall interviewing Sigurd Olson up in Ely, Minnesota, a few years back, and hearing him tell of the days he guided back in the northern Minnesota-Ontario bush country.

"I used to be amused," he said, "when I'd come back in from a trip and usually the first questions from the people in town were: 'Well, how did you do? Did you catch any big ones?' "

Sigurd said he would ask: *What big ones?* and they would say *Didn't you do any fishing?*

"Oh," Sigurd would tell them, "we did fish a couple of times."

His listeners would be greatly disappointed, Sigurd chuckled. They couldn't *imagine* going back into the bush without going in to fish. Sigurd said he always figured that if those townspeople had gone back into the wilderness and stayed long enough, they might discover something different from fishing.

"Intangible values," Sigurd smiled, "that's what we're talking about. Values that are difficult to explain."

He said these intangibles were sacred, as opposed to secular. He said the Indians had sensed them long before we were here.

"They had their sacred places," Sigurd said, "where they didn't speak, just as we have them in our great cathedrals and in our places of worship."

Almost everyone who fishes knows that Izaak Walton is the patron saint of all anglers, but not everyone knows that in

England's Winchester Cathedral there's a stained-glass window dedicated to him.

In the base of that window, Sigurd Olson points out, are four words that embody the philosophy of all who enjoy the gentle art of fishing and the out-of-doors:

STUDY TO BE QUIET

Sigurd says that's the key to all Ike ever wrote and thought about. Beside the rivers Itchen and Dove, Izaak Walton fished for peace and quiet, seeking the silences and the places where thoughts were long and undisturbed.

You seek out the silence, the quiet, and then you listen for Something. You simply *listen*.

"Almost everything is listening for something," Sig Olson concluded. "It is part of the hunger all of us have for a time when we were closer to nature than we are today."

Perhaps that's why we don't take so many fish poles along anymore. We're really just listening for Something.

"Well, while you're waiting to hear," says Steady Eddy, "take extra poppers for the bluegills."

Finding Buck's Lake

"**F**ishermen are a perverse and restless lot," Judge John Voelker, also known as Robert Traver, observed in his book *Trout Madness*, "constantly poised to migrate to greener pastures, ever helpless recruits for the wild goose chase."

I was thinking of the Good Wise Judge in Upper Michigan because down here in Lower Wisconsin, the crafty Hugh Percy was telling about the green pasture and I was poised to migrate. Inwardly. Outwardly, I sipped the instant garage coffee that could unseize rusted-up bolts, and tried not to look at all like a helpless recruit.

"They're apt to be up and away at the drop of an idle rumor," the Judge had characterized fisherpersons. "Indeed, this willingness to pursue the will-o'-the-wisp—this curious readiness to chase bubbles, mirages, and rainbows up and down the land—seems to make up half the lure of fishing."

41

The Judge had been talking about *trout* fishing in particular, and today Hugh Percy was not talking trout fishing in particular, but the Judge had us down pat.

"Some wild-eyed mosquito-crazed character," the Judge had warned, "sidles up to another fisherman and furtively mumbles, I just heard of a place where they splash waves in your face—and off they zoom to the moon, gaily negotiating seven cedar swamps on the way."

"They say the bluegills up there," Perce was saying, "are the biggest ones you've ever seen. Big as your hand. Big as a small frying pan."

I could picture the little lake back in the boonies, a mile's hike from the overgrown sand road, the shallows, reedy and clear as wellwater. I pictured wading the eastern shore with a flyrod and casting the tiny black popper into the red sunset.

"*Buck* Lake," Perce was saying, "or *Bucks* Lake. Or Buck's Lake. I don't think it's on the map, but I think I can find it."

God, I wanted to believe.

Buck's Lake made the most sense. I intuited that the original Buck was not a white-tailed deer but probably a local guide who stumbled upon this little gem when he was prospecting for walleyes or looking for a good minnow lake, or maybe just a place to skinny-dip. The monster bluegills were a bonus. Buck was probably in the veterans' home at King. Or buried. Or long-gone to Alaska because his country filled up.

God, *how* I wanted to believe.

"I could get the camper ready," Perce was saying. "We could go up and have a look-see."

I thought of all the times I had gone along with somebody to have a look-see at great fishing waters. Trout water. Bass water. Musky water. Walleye water. Sacred, all of it. Sacred and secret, and most of it lying Back of Beyond.

There was the secret trout pond back in the boonies discovered by Jimmy White's father, and he swore us to secrecy because it was full of wild brook trout and not even the Indians knew about it. All the way up in the midnight drive of Opening Day, he kept chortling in the back seat about how you really had to have a nose for trout water, and how there was plenty of smarts in the Old Dog yet, because without him, us Young Pups wouldn't find good brookie water unless we fell into it.

He also kept saying that this pond was a little piece of heaven and if something happened to him, he wouldn't mind just being buried there.

"Something happens to me today," he sighed throughout the trip, "just leave me up here and tell your Mother."

He slept then and Jimmy shook his head and drove, finally waking the Old Dog at the designated turnoff. We bumped in for a half mile, parked in the alder and walked in the rest of the way. We reached the pond about the same time as the first light of dawn, and saw, drawn up around the banks, shoulder to shoulder and wall to wall, an army of fisherpersons beating the waters to a lather.

The Old Dog's mouth fell open like an empty creel.

"Today," Jimmy said finally to the Old Dog, "today could be the day that something happens to you."

"Any fisherman," Judge Voelker ruled, "with red fish blood in his veins has himself made these wild excursions, only to return, flushed and fishless, when the day is far spent, smelling of strong drink, and the truth is not in him.

"All of us are guilty. Fishermen who no longer heed these siren calls have either become ex-fishermen or old fishermen."

"The lake's probably full of stunted little bluegills," Hugh Percy was saying, "if it's there at all. But don't you just want to go look for it?"

"We could go look," I said.

"What could it hurt?" Perce said.

Finding that lake would be great.

So would not finding it.

Catalog

*I*n the very way that Jerry Minnich finds harbingers of Spring in his seed catalogs, many of us—driven from the Garden at birth because of our brown thumbs—find the same promise of warmth and open waters in the arrival of our fishing catalogs.

This year especially, with a Winter cold enough to frost you, your pocketbook, and your plumbing in one shot, it's a sight for snowblind eyes to find the Orvis catalog in your mail-box. It's finding a trillium there. Or a trout lily. Or a trout.

The catalog arrived the other morning, eternal and constant as the snows of winter and the streams of spring, *ORVIS, 126 Years of Sporting Tradition* emblazoned on the cover along with the emblems of that tradition, the trout rod and the trout net among them.

For those of us who haunt the Catfish Flats and are apt to do more fishing with flywheels than flyrods, the Orvis catalog is not just a thing of beauty. It is exotic beyond our wildest dreams. Coral reefs give you this kind of high. And Canadian rivers. Marco Polo must have had a similar inventory:

• The Wes Jordan bamboo flyrods made of select Tonkin cane from Kwangsi Province in China.

• The exquisite fly reels—for every kind of fishing under this earth's sun—from ultra-light Battenkills to heavy-duty Fin-Nors.

• Pages and pages of color plates—dry flies, wet flies, nymphs, streamers, bugs—enough pages for the Brenton boys up on the Big Stone to repaper the whole little cabin, right over the Vilas County News Review.

It was all kind of familiar until I turned a page, and there—suddenly, surprisingly—was something I had never encountered in the Orvis catalog. Rounding the bend, the rapids you heard isn't a rapids at all. It's a waterfall.

This waterfall was a two-page spread titled "The Orvis Fisherman is not always a man." Below that, the management had written: "In response to our distaff anglers' request for fishing gear made especially for women, we present a selection of equipment and appropriate attire chosen with function, comfort and appearance in mind."

There followed a list of fishing items designed for women—from Orvis Gumbottoms to Orvis Tac-L-Pac vests.

There were also female models shown, standing at the brink of gin-clear trout water wearing specially cut Ladies' Deluxe Waders and Ladies' Felt Sole Hip Boots.

Permit me to observe that Orvis is performing a great service to everyone by noting, at long last, that fishing is not an exclusively masculine pursuit.

One day, perhaps, it will also be noted that long before men were writing about fishing—men like Nick Lyons, Ernest

Schwiebert, Ernest Hemingway, Joe Brooks, Lee Wulff—fishermen from A. J. McLane to Zane Grey, *including* Ike Walton— a singular woman wrote about fishing first. And what she wrote remains a classic to this day.

If Izaak Walton is the Big Daddy of fishing because he wrote *The Compleat Angler*, then Dame Juliana Berners is the Big Mama, because she wrote *The Treatise Of Fysshynge Wyth An Angle*. The spelling looks funny because Dame Juliana was writing way back in 1496.

She is to angling literature, Arnold Gingrich states in his book, *The Fishing in Print: A Guided Tour Through Five Centuries of Angling Literature*, as Chaucer is to English literature. Each represents, to all intents and purposes, the very beginning.

No one knows for certain whether Dame Juliana was indeed the abbess of a convent, or why she wrote *The Treatise*, or even *if* she wrote it for certain. Her trail disappears into the misty past like the headwaters of some fabled stream.

I believe. The Dame is real. Before she gets down to the fishing, she writes the following as a little preface:

> . . . if a man lacks physicians or doctors, he shall make three things his doctors or physicians, and he will never have need of more.
> The first of them is merry thought.
> The second is work in moderation.
> The third is a good diet of pure foods and suitable drinks.

Steady Eddy agrees you follow advice like that to hell and back.

When she gets into the fishing, it could be Sig Olson's Grandma, or yours, talking:

> You must not use this artful sport for covetousness, merely for the increasing or saving of your money, but mainly for your enjoyment and to procure the health of your body and, more especially, of your soul. For when you intend to go to your amusements in fishing, you will not want very many persons with you who might hinder you in your pastime.

45

You talk about relating and communicating despite a generation gap. Dame Juliana was writing this stuff almost 500 years ago, and it reads like this month's *Outdoor Life*. She warns:

> Also you must not be too greedy in catching your said game, as in taking too much at one time, a thing which can easily happen if you do in every point as this treatise shows you. That could easily be the occasion of destroying your own sport and other men's also. When you have a sufficient mess, you should covet no more at that time. . . . And all those that do according to this rule will have the blessing of God. . . .

Dame Juliana did fisherpersons a great, great service. It's only fitting and meet that fisherpersons are starting to return the favor.

The Legacy

*T*he last time I had seen Mabel Mueller, her husband was still alive and they were living in retirement on a lake north of Boulder Junction.

Now John was gone and Mabel's note came from southern Illinois, where she was living with her older daughter.

Her younger daughter, Nancy, married my wife's younger brother, and they had visited from Massachusetts last summer.

Steady Eddy says it's kind of like watching "As the World Turns."

"Nancy mentioned to me," Mabel wrote in that careful way people write when they were raised with inkwells and pen wipers and the Palmer Method, "that you would like a fishing hook or two . . . "

I remembered the bluebird day, when John had taken us down the winding main channel of the flowage, the outboard throttled to a gurgling, one rod rigged for largemouth bass, the other for northern pike. The fishing turned out to be slow, but the sloughs were alive with ospreys.

". . . so I asked my grandson, Billy, who had gotten my husband's fishing box, about it. Billy said he would be glad to share a few with you. Since he is only eleven, he won't be fishing much for a while. The hooks need polishing though. Well, happy fishing trails."

She concluded by saying they were doing "pretty well" in southern Illinois and that the weather was beautiful right now, but the hot summer months are "pretty bad."

Enclosed were a homemade weedless yellow bucktail, a red and white Millsite "Bassor" Floater, and a beat-up, tarnished Johnson Silver Minnow.

God bless, little Billy. There's a lot of Grandpa Mueller in you.

I began writing Billy a thank-you note in my head.

Dear Billy, it went. *Thank you for sharing your Grandpa Mueller's fishing tackle with me. It's hard to put down on paper all the thoughts that are running through my head as I look at these real treasures that were so much a part of your Grandpa and now are part of us, too.*

One of the thoughts running through my head was the sense that that little box of artifacts could have been any box, any packet sent home from any of the world's battlefields; watches and rings and lifeless things left behind by someone who didn't need them anymore, by someone who was traveling light now, by someone who had raced ahead of us all in the plodding caravan, free of things, free as the wind, free at last. Personal Effects. The relics of saints. I fingered that yellow bucktail the way I used to finger my rosary, and I could see John casting this very thing over the flowage, far over the years.

The yellow bucktail in my hand was of the same alchemy. A talisman. A shaman's magic. To touch it is to be changed. To touch it is to travel time itself.

One day Billy would understand all this better than anyone. There was no need to put it down on paper now.

"You muddy the water," Steady says, "and nobody feels like drinking it."

I thought it made more sense to tell Billy that his Grandpa had a lot in common with Sigurd Olson's Grandma. As he wrote in his book, *The Singing Wilderness*:

> Grandmother and I had things in common: a certain sense of adventure regarding the taking of a mess of speck-

47

les, an intuitive agreement that there was nothing more important than fishing in the spring and nothing more beautiful than a speckle fresh from the creek. We knew about such matters as the smell of bursting buds and thawing earth, the calling of whippoorwills at dusk, and the afterglow of sunsets. She shared every joy that was mine, and I loved her for it as only a small boy can who has found perfect companionship. From her, I know, I inherited my feeling and love for the wild places of this earth.

I lifted the Silver Minnow out of the box. Mabel was right—it could use some polishing. It took me back to those misspent summers on the Chain of Lakes when, bareheaded and brown beyond burning, I could whip a big Silver Minnow and pork-rind all day long in the tea-brown sloughs and never feel it the next morning. No twinges. Nor arthritic fingers. Just plain youth. Day after day.

It reminded me of a piece Howard Walden had in *Fly Fisherman* magazine: He wrote that nearly forty years ago, long before his grandson was born, an old fisherman he knew phoned him to come over.

"I've been thinking," the old fisherman said, "that I'll never fish again. I have here in my attic a collection of trout gear so extensive as to be vulgar. If it stays here it will die of dry rot and inertia. I'm rounding up some young blood to exercise it and I'm starting with you. Come over and pick out as many items as you can use."

Walden says it evoked a new, strange emotion in him; the deliberate surrender of fishing to the facts of old age, to the fact of death. . . .

His grandson was seventeen when Howard Walden invited him to pick through the gear and take what he wanted.

The little Winchester rod. A Hardy Perfect Reel. A pair of stocking-foot waders from Scotland. . . .

Howard is gone now, but his gear is still fishing. Like John Mueller's, except for the box Billy sent. I put it with my father's stuff. That's unpolished, too.

The TT&SSC

S ome folks bowl together weekly. Some folks golf together. Some folks even get together once a week for more sedentary activities like bridge, bingo, foosball, and potluck suppers.

Delbert and Ed and Zeke have gotten together every Thursday for years and they fish. Specifically, they fish for trout, stream trout, trout that live in the rivers and the "cricks" west of Madison.

With the trout season about to end, and with prior commitments on the part of two-thirds of the membership for Thursday, it was determined that the Last Day would be moved ahead to Tuesday and that yours truly be permitted to attend as Nonpaying Guest of the management in general and of Delbert in particular.

Thus did I come to be an Honorary Member in Good Standing of the Thursday Trouting and Squirreltail Social Club, an organization based on the same brand of youthful optimism that sustained us back in the halcyon days when we set bowling pins by hand in the basement of Holy Assumption parish hall and occasionally used our feet to prod Old Man Clancy's wobbly spares into miraculously big beer frames.

Hard losers were heard to say behind Clancy's back that because of his clutch performances—which defied not only all logic but even on one occasion, the Law of Gravity itself—that the only appropriate lettering for his bowling shirt was simply: LOURDES.

Clancy's Bowling, like Clancy's Church, became a ritual for us, but no more so I would guess than the procedures followed by the TT&SSC.

It wasn't exactly bluebird weather. It was gray and overcast and it looked more than a little like rain later on.

Delbert drove, picking up Ed first in his quiet neighborhood, and then Zeke, in his quiet neighborhood, their little bundles of gear piled at curbside, flyrods rigged but unjointed, hipboots, vests, raingear, lunches, and the funkiest-looking lived-in Arctic Creels you've ever seen.

I was struck by their close-shaven faces, their neatly pressed shirts, and their pants that didn't bag at all. I didn't look that presentable when I was attending Clancy's Church.

In a restaurant booth, you would take them for anything but fishermen. Retired letter carriers, perhaps. FBI agents. Professors on sabbatical.

We stopped for the second cup of coffee and doughnuts, a traditional stop, and socialized a little.

Ed complained about IRS, Madison Gas & Electric and computer billing, not necessarily in that order. Zeke figured that only a Philadelphia lawyer could now understand his electric bill because lawyers from all over had screwed it up in the first place. Del pretty much agreed, leaving the distinct impression that this was not the most conservative chapter of flyfisherpersons around. They also insisted on picking up my tab.

We drove west for a long way and then north and then west again.

Del stopped at a bridge and we all stretched and got into our boots and looked at the river, a no-keep, for-fun-only, river.

The water was muddy brown and cloudy. Del said he and I would fish upstream to the next bridge. Ed and Zeke could take the car, fish up above and meet us at the bridge for lunch.

I caught the first fish. A very small one. On one of Del's Bombers, a hand-tied girdlebug. And then I caught the first hipboot. A very large one. On a strand of barbed wire strung on the very first fence. They were old boots, weathered out on top, on their last legs anyway and now the left one was slashed to ribbons and as much protection against the cold water as a garter-belt.

"It's the Last Day," Del observed. "Especially for that boot."

I squished all the way up to the next bridge, detained by only one brown along the way, and pausing every now and again to marvel at the way Del whipped the graphite rod into fluid flowing patterns that magically caused trout to appear attached to the fly. Watching him catch fish was surpassed only by watching him release fish. They were labors of love.

For a lot of folks, Del said, fishing, like hunting, like a lot of other activities in this life, was only fun if you got to keep *Something*. Putting a big trout back—or a little trout for that matter—struck some folks as just plain dumb and stupid. It strikes the locals that way and they're raising hell with the Department of Natural Resources.

After lunch, we drove to another stream where you get to keep what you catch and Del got a brown and the other members got a brown and I got no fish.

I merely got to squish past a beaver dam. Past a pack of hounds treeing a coon in the smoky-gold hills. Past a flock of bluebirds fluttering and sitting the fenceposts of the last meadow. That's not exactly coming up empty.

The bluebirds were leaving, even as the TT&SSC was leaving, until next Spring.

The members of the TT&SSC would settle in for Winter and tie up dozens of Bombers and Squirreltails for their next Outing. Del. And Ed. And Zeke.

I have a hunch that in their own quiet ways, they could be as much fun as Clancy's bowling team. I have to find out if the TT&SSC ever takes in new members. Hell, I could be their whole bohunk quota. And shaving every Thursday is probably good for you anyway. Also I'd be more than happy to get my bowling shirt re-lettered.

Fish Management

We were on a fishing trip the other day to Bud Jordahl's farm in the Richland County hills.

You would never get Bud, though, to tell you that what we were doing was primarily fishing. Bud would tell you that what we were doing, primarily, was "research." That's because Bud is a professor at the University of Wisconsin and professors talk that way.

He had noticed that his bass ponds "seemed to need a little pruning," and that's why Jordie and Steve and I were along—to "prune."

Jordie is Bud's son. Steve Born, also a professor, is Bud's special outdoors friend who knows all about water hydrology and who refers to himself in polite company as "a bohunk from Chicago." My credentials, while not as impressive, are at least acceptable in water-blessed fiefdoms like this enchanted hill-country farm. I filet pretty good and will volunteer my services at the drop of a honing stone.

It is honorable work and in any team sport would surely be listed as one of the "skill positions."

In the pond called Twin Pines—the one that needed "particular pruning"—Bud had stocked "ten or fifteen" largemouth bass three years ago. They had multiplied like guppies, feeding mostly on the resident snails, Bud figured, "and the bigger ones are probably eating the littler ones" because Bud had not done the traditional thing and stocked bluegills along with the bass.

"The fisheries guys," Bud said, "say that you can mix bluegills and bass and the bass will feed on the bluegills. Well, we tried that in a different pond, and we found that the bass can't really keep up with the bluegill population, and eventually, inevitably, you wind up with a stunted population that's competing for the same food base."

He says the alternatives, if you really want to go with the bluegills, are to stock either all males or all females so they can't reproduce. He also says: Good Luck.

"I don't know how to sex them," he admits, "and if you miss on the sex identification, boom! You've got that population explosion. Then you're into the stunted fish cycle again and you're going to have to restock."

"Put a musky in the pond," Jordie says, "and that should take care of the stunted bluegills. I'd even settle for a northern pike."

"You can easily see," Steady Eddy would say later, "that there is yet another researcher in the Prof's family."

"I was going to stock smallmouth bass," Bud said, "but they need gravel spawning beds, and there is no gravel in the pond, so you'd have to construct spawning beds for them. But why go to all that management when the largemouth bass reproduce in the pond as is and it seems to fit right in with the natural scheme of things here?"

Why, indeed? As you used to hear in the 400 Bar before they stopped the trains and closed the depot: *If it ain't broke, don't fix it.*

Part of the natural scheme, Bud points out, is that when largemouth bass spawn, the female will deposit 1,500 eggs in one nest. Of that number 1,000 will hatch into fry. Of the 1,000 fry, 250 will survive, which vindicates the Prof's environmental practice on the pond. You could be up to here in bass.

"Unless you prune them," he says, "they'll eat themselves out of house and home, and then Ma Nature will prune them for you."

Bud, Jordie, and Steve fished the big pond from a boat. Actually, only Jordie and Steve really fished. Bud rowed them around, and as they got into fish he looked as proud as the country boy giving a couple of city visitors their first tractor ride around the alfalfa.

"I always wanted to be a farmer," he confessed. "That's all I ever wanted to be."

All over the pond, the fishing was astounding. Foot long bass were common. Jordie hooked and lost one that everybody acknowledged was really big. Jordie swears "at least twenty inches." Bud says that's the beauty part when they get away.

After supper, Steve and I tried the little pond just beyond the house. By the time I walked to the far side, he was onto a fish. It seemed heavy, then it bored into the weeds and hung him up. Steve pulled on the rod, banged on the butt handle. Easy. Hard. Nothing happened. Maybe it was the falling darkness, maybe the frustration. He forced the rod. The line tightened, stretched, *pinged*, snapped. He stared, then started taking off his clothes.

"The line's all coiled up on top of the water," he yelled. "I'm going in."

I cranked in my Creme worm, my heart beating faster. He stripped down to his shorts, waded out tentatively, body tense, shoulders hunched, the way you do sinking in goo. Then he was swimming. He reached the line, submerged, came up, and called that he'd located the fish. When he submerged again, the quiet was awful. I could hear the Sheriff saying that bohunks shouldn't be permitted around farm ponds, especially in pairs. I was practically running when Steve emerged, no longer tense. Hand-over-hand, he hauled in the fat largemouth. Fourteen inches, but deep. Steve laughed as he pulled his dry clothes on over his wet shorts. I told him he could have taken off his shorts and they'd be dry now too. He said he would have, only he was afraid of turtles.

We climbed the fence and a herd of Aldo Leopold's black-and-white buffalo followed us home.

Cleaning Fish

*T*he white plastic five-gallon pail just sat there on the patio stones, beading with moisture and drawing me with its promise.

I sharpened the Rapala filet knife and counted myself among the most fortunate of mortals because of the pail's contents, and because those contents were all mine.

"At this point," Steady Eddy likes to tell The Indian, "you would think all this excitement is being generated by some exotic treat within the pail, right—some treat that turns on most people in these civilized parts? Maybe ice cream? Maybe cold beer?"

I have learned to shut out the triumph in Steady's voice.

"Dead fish," he tells The Indian. "The pail is full of dead fish. To the brim."

"Dead fish?"

I have learned to shut out The Indian, too.

"He *likes* to clean fish?" he tells Steady.

"That's what I'm telling you," Steady says.

"Somebody's got to do it," The Indian says, "but you don't have to *like* it."

Well, Steady and The Indian are wrong. I do not *like* to clean fish. *I love to clean fish.* Cleaning fish is one of the great things The Old Man taught me. Along with drawing the cueball. Playing position. And always leaving your opponent on the rail.

The Old Man used to say that catching fish was only half of it; cleaning fish was the other half. He started me out pretty early and I helped him clean, and after a few years, he was helping me clean, and after a few more years, I got to do it all myself.

I can't pinpoint the day it started to be a joy, but it was during those pine-winey summer days on the shores of the Big Stone Lake when the stringers were full of walleyes, cold and golden-brown and plump as suckers. We each had a limit, seven

54

fish apiece—I think he caught them all—each fish over the fifteen-inch size limit, and as I cut into them, I just suddenly knew that what I was doing was a joyful thing and there was nowhere else I wanted to be at that moment and nothing else I wanted to do. Not even going back on the rock bar and catching walleyes. I was content to clean, to *be in the flow*, as the Buddhists say, and to understand what was happening with the sharp knife and the firm flesh; to understand what was happening to the fish because of me and what was happening to me because of the fish.

And *why*.

I stopped going to church the same year. Maybe there's no connection, but I did spend most of the summer back in the marshes fishing—Sundays, too—and Father Himmelsbach finally shook his head and gave up on me.

I remember telling Tom Helmer and Guy Lewis that I loved to clean fish when we went up to Algoma a couple of autumns back, and Tom gracefully let me filet four chinooks, two of them around twenty-five pounds apiece, the dark blood along the backbones deep and set in the consistency of Jell-O.

Tom's in Atlanta now, but I may send him a page from a new book by Elizabeth Arthur, who, with her husband, lived on an island up in British Columbia. She wrote something on fishing which I wish I had written, because this says it all.

"A long time ago," she writes in *Island Sojourn*, "I caught my first trout, a nineteen-inch rainbow. I was standing in a milky lake, aqua blue with glacial silt. I did not want to catch the fish. He needn't have taken my casting seriously. The day was, I thought, far too rarefied for action; too many years lay calmly on the shore. Suddenly, he was on my line; he wanted to come in. We had a bit of a tussle, but I dragged him to the shore and flipped him onto a rock. There he lay, and his eyes grew clouded, troubled. I wanted to throw him back, but quite suddenly, I couldn't move. I felt in the presence of a catastrophic power, his eye like a window of the earth, calmly staring at me, slowly misting over. Somewhere deep within the eye there was a leer which said, *You call yourself a creature. Ha. Kill me if you wish to be anything at all. Kill me before you melt at my feet.*

"I picked him up and smashed his head in. The colors of his skin glinted as he jerked, convulsed like the eruption of a volcano.

"The air around me crystallized; the trees rustled in kind applause. Later I cooked the fish.

"He's still a part of me."

I'd like Tom Helmer to read that page, not to mention every man, woman and child who has ever dropped a line into the great mysteries below the surfaces of the eternal waters and waited with expectancy and excitement and wonder.

Speaking of which, it may be time to get out on The Catfish Flats with Steady Eddy, and wait with all of the above. Plus chunk baits.

"Now," says Steady, "*now*, we are talking exotic treats."

Old Timers

*T*he Opening Day of the new trout season is a ritual in our neck of the woods.

You lay out all your gear in the hallway and wait for Don Reinfeldt to pick you up after midnight. Your wife, having witnessed this annual madness for years, performs with all the aloof professionalism of a SAC pilot running through the pre-flight check list. Coffee—plenty. Sandwiches—liver sausage, Bananas—a pair.

The radio warns of rainshowers and you know darned well she checked the creel to make sure the raingear is rolled up therein. By the time Don arrives, she has you so organized there is time to share a cup of coffee and savor the holiday feeling.

Later, in the headlight beams, the highway strips away like line from a reel. The city thins out and the country begins. Fencelines, red barns, cattle crossings. Sleeping farms and watchful dogs. Driving to a trout stream in the middle of the night may not be the greatest joy of this life. But it is one of them.

After the first hour, the land changes. Slowly, subtly.

There are more pines now. There is naked sand in the cutbanks. The northern forest begins here. You leave the main highway and follow the secondary roads.

A startled rabbit veers across the road and plunges into the brush. You observe that it was a skinny rabbit and Don hopes that it will live long enough to be a fat one by Fall.

The pasturelands are rock-strewn here. Deserted, weathered, collapsed buildings stand mournfully along the road. A crumbled, blackened, fieldstone foundation marks the spot where a barn once stood. Did fire get it? Don says the whole countryside burned over once. It's great berry country later on.

Another hour passes and Don swings onto the last turnoff before the stream. Before he finishes his cigaret, you will be there.

As you climb the last rise and roll toward the little bridge, you count the darkened cars on the shoulder. Two. Three. And two more. Counting yours, that's six. You won't be shoulder to shoulder on the stream.

You cross the bridge and you can hear the water gurgling below. It looks good, Don says, and you agree. It always looks good.

Parked off the road, you step into the wet grass and feel the North Country chill on your face.

You also smell pine and the stream and the hot coffee.

From the other direction, beams of light ignite the ground fog like a fire. In five minutes, a car parks opposite you, the engine stops, and Norm Zimmerman walks over. You have your coffee and talk and dress for the stream and talk some more until the false dawn lightens the eastern sky.

It reminds you of the army when you all got up quietly and talked softly and then each man moved out with his own thoughts.

For the next half-day, you will only catch glimpses of the others. Shadowy. In the brush. Back from the streambank. Miles from here. There will be no motors. No boats. There will be very little sign of man.

There will be only this wilderness stream and you.

Alone with your thoughts.

THROUGH THE ICE

Fishing Through the Roof

I never really believe that Winter is here until I see it from the cattail marsh.

One day, the bay beyond is alive with ducks, dabbling and gabbling in their footloose formations without a care in this world.

And the very next day, the bay is silent with skim ice, the ducks gone to open water and the cold settling into place like poured concrete.

Now, I believe.

You can't walk on this ice yet, but in a matter of a few weeks, there will be a well-traveled trail, a beaten-down path, laced with Vibram-soled bootprints and the tracks of icefishing sleds.

On a clear day, from this very point, you will be able to distinguish, out on the roof of the lake, the bulky, quilted figures of the tribal elders. The Olson clan: Randy, Buck, Greg, Tom, Jim Thrun, the legendary bass Hunter and Catcher, not

59

to mention the immortal Vince Colletti, and his Magical Mystery Tour Sled.

They will encamp like some advance party accustomed to freezing planets, disdaining all shelters and tents—unless you count the canvas windbreak on Colletti's sled—their territory staked out by the skyblue Mora augers, sitting on their plastic pails with the green and orange iceflies, the jigging poles and tipups, the Golden Rapalas and silver Swedish Pimples, the spikes and Susans.

They will all be out there, happy as penguins, doing the simplest, yet perhaps the hardest, of all fishing: fishing through the ice. Fishing, as Steady Eddy likes to put it, through the roof.

The thing about icefishing is that it can be a social event, if you wish, or it can be isolation, and if you are talking isolation, being *alone* out on the ice, then you are talking about something mystical, something very elemental and primal, something that the Old Time People understood a lot better than we do.

In many American Indian cultures, the poet-naturalist Gary Snyder observed in *Earth House Hold*, it is obligatory for every member to get out of the society, out of the human nexus, and "out of his head" at least once in his life. He returns from his solitary vision-quest with a secret name, a protective animal spirit, a secret song. It is his "power." The culture honors the person who has visited other realms.

Peyote, mushrooms, morning glory seeds, and Jimson weed are some of the best-known herbal aids used by Indian cultures to assist in the quest.

"Most tribes," Snyder says, "apparently achieved these results through yogic-type disciplines: sweatbaths, hours of dancing, fasting and total isolation."

For many people, he says, the invisible presence of the Indian, and the heartbreaking beauty of America, work without fasting or herbs.

"We make these contacts," he concludes, "simply by walking the Sierra or Mohave . . . and watching . . ."

"And you can throw in," Steady adds, "any North Country lake after Christmas."

There's a whole different breed of folks on the ice who would scoff if you called them spiritual, or meditative, or anything but practical nonvisionaries out for perch, and most of them have never heard of J. Krishnamurti at all, but the Old Guru had heard of them all right, and he had them figured.

The ecstasy of solitude, Krishnamurti says, comes when you are not frightened to be alone; no longer belonging to the world or attached to anything.

"Then, like the dawn that came up this morning," he writes, "it comes silently and makes a golden path in the very stillness, which was at the beginning, which is now, and which will always be there."

Close your eyes and you could be in the high Himalayas. Open your eyes and it's Tibet.

The Seven-Foot Nun

*I*t came to me on the ice the other day: a kind of vision the shamans have.

The wind raised great snow devils on the field of ice. They rose and dropped, and you could follow the waves of crystals as they flowed across the ice like some living force on the face of a dead planet. As the waves passed over my ice-beaded Sorel boots, I felt an invisible cold on my face and then it was gone, and I was toasty warm everywhere else as usual.

I wriggled my toes in the ice-crusted boots and hung out with my feet; dry, warm, hibernating in their little cocoons of wool socks and felt liners, and the rubber-leather miracles that were as warm as igloos.

That's when it came to me. *The vision.*

I looked at my feet and saw them the way they were all the winters I was growing up. They weren't encased in Sorel boots. They were encased in the knee-high clammy constructions called High Cuts. God, I shivered at the thought, and I realized that a whole generation of us had grown up with wet, cold, clammy feet in those damned leather boots because they gave away a pocket knife with the boots and we all convinced our mothers that the boots were the best thing since Wonder Bread.

61

We wore high cuts and corduroy knickers, and we all should have perished in the snows of yesteryear except for a basic law of life. As Dynie Mansfield always put it: *The good Lord watches over the Dumb Ones.*

And Catholic kids weren't the only ones.

George Schaller, in his book *Stones of Silence*, an account of his journeys in the Himalayas, writes of thinly clad Sherpas, one in knickers and tennis shoes "like a school boy on a picnic."

"I tell him to put on his boots," Schaller reports, "but he replies that he has no boots, that the money I gave him to buy a pair in Kathmandu was spent on other things. To cross passes nearly 18,000 feet high in midwinter in tennis shoes is a good way to freeze toes, I note dourly, and hand him my last clean pair of wool socks."

Calvin Rutstrum thinks we have a "cold and snow fear complex," and he says that most people try to avoid Winter altogether by either staying inside the house or heading for the warmer climates.

"As a boy," Rutstrum boasts in his book *Paradise Below Zero*:

> I experienced great exhilaration on the arrival of winter. After more than half a century, I have not lost it. While perhaps for wholesome acceptance of winter one needs a healthy, robust body that craves vigorous action and diversion from the too often physically enervating, comfortable norm, what seems the most important requirement of all is an understanding of the physiological relationship of mind and body as it adapts to the little-understood exigencies of cold and snow.

What all that means, Steady says, is that grade school kids make angels in the snow and high school kids wear tennies in the snow and Old Guys still wear their funny, heatless snap-brim hats like their fathers before them.

Seventy to eighty per cent of your body heat, the experts say, can be lost through your head.

"And if you've got a big head," Steady shrugs, "God only knows. . ."

Inside the thermal underwear, inside the windproof snowmobile suit, I watched the pictures inside my head.

There we are, in the seventh grade, Charlie Kaiser and all the rest of us, sopping wet and smelling like wet feathers, rosy-cheeked and runny-nosed, the radiators hissing, the wooden floors creaking, the smell of damp in the air, of leather, wool and corduroy; the Seven-Foot Nun noting any deviation from the norm—a handful of snow saved from Outside, an icicle, saved and shoved under someone's dry seat or down someone's dry neck. Devil's work. She always saw Charlie clearly, and Charlie behind his thick glasses had to cock his head and squint when he tried to see her at all.

The Seven-Foot Nun always stood outside the boys' john, supervising our entry and egress, four boys at a time, because there were four urinals (and for the longest time in that innocent age we never knew how she knew that) and not too much time dawdling or "monkey business."

Charlie, first free spirit we ever knew, like a puppy put out to piddle, loved to rush around in there, flushing all the johns in sequence, ratcheting down all the paper towel dispensers, running water in all the sinks and generally creating an uproar.

He would giggle insanely, as outside the Seven-Foot Nun warned, then pleaded, then cajoled, then threatened and then—one unforgettable day, she not only did all that, *she also walked into the john, grabbed Charlie by the ear, and marched us all out.*

Shocked. Shaken. Never to be secure again.

Now, *that. That* was a cold day.

Bluegills

"**G**od must have loved the common bluegill, because She made so many of them."

She certainly made a big batch of them for Lake Wingra and they all looked like they were stamped out in a button factory.

They were itty-bitty fishies, just barely bite-sized, the most impressive of them hardly bigger than poker chips.

Well, I've been fishing Wingra with a great deal of intensity this Winter, sometimes alone, sometimes in the warming company of other assorted nuts, and we're here to tell you that the Button Bluegills—the "kivver" minnows as Charlie Bran calls them—no longer dominate the Wingra fishery as they once did.

The Wingra bluegills are getting bigger. Granted, they aren't in the Squaw Bay class yet, and the Old Pro from Waubesa still looks at you like your ears are loose, but the bluegills in Wingra are getting bigger than they used to get. And I've got witnesses.

Vince Coletti. And his Magical Mystery Tour sled. All members of the Olson clan and others, honorary and in good standing. Even Jim Thrun after drilling two dozen "dry holes" last weekend wound up prospecting for panfish.

Everybody agrees: More little bluegills are growing up. And more big people are happy about that than you can shake a jigging stick at.

I think everybody's happy about it except me.

Oh, sure. I know the way the argument goes: Bigger bluegills mean better fishing because now they'll be worth keeping and cleaning. Hell, I always kept and cleaned—fileted, yet— the itty-bitty ones. They taste as good—better—than the big ones.

I always agreed with the Old Weed Eater and Wild Asparagus Stalker, Euell Gibbons when he discoursed on the peewee bluegill:

> Everyone agrees that the bluegill is delicious, but very few think it is worth the effort required to clean, cook and pick the meat from the bones. I don't agree. To me, cleaning, cooking and eating bluegills is an essential part of the pleasure I derive from this colorful little fish. Properly cleaning a bluegill is an art well worth learning. I not only clean and skin them, I filet them. Yes, I really do, and I'm not a surgeon either. My whole family considers these little half ounce filets the finest fish I ever bring home.

Right on, Euell! I even *scale* the teensy-weensy ones leaving the skin on because the skin is what holds the meat together.

"Waste not, want not," The Old Man used to say in another place and in another language.

Bigger bluegills also mean bigger crowds. Aye. There's the rub. The word is out and the crowds are coming. They're a different breed and they're changing the old neighborhood.

There's even a guy out there with a power auger for God's sake. He drills more holes than Thrun but it's like meditating in the cathedral when the skybus roars over.

You don't need the eyes of an eagle to see what's coming next. So, I'm going to find a pond, a puddle where the bluegills are so small nobody in his right mind would fish for them. And I'm going to fish for them. All Winter long.

And when people ask me where I've been all Winter I'll tell them I went back to work.

A Nose for Ice Fishing

Steady Eddy calls them "the folks who fish the hardwater." They wear thermal underwear, drill holes in the ice until it looks like a prairie dog colony, and are unashamed to admit they use maggots for bait.

They're in their element right now, contemplating the Buddha at the Bottom-of-the-Lake and doing their thing on the glacier.

"You don't have to be crazy to go ice fishing," Steady Eddy preaches down at the bait shop, "but it doesn't hurt."

It could even help a little.

What normal person is going to trudge out onto the ice in freezing temperatures, drill a hole, and then sit there contemplating it for hours on end, day after day, month after month?

"No normal person," Steady concedes. "Just us."

I always figured that The Old Man's rationale was as good as any I ever heard.

"With our big noses," he used to say of his tribe, "we are natural-born ice fishermen."

The Old Man held the theory that broad noses and economy-sized nostrils preheated the North Country air so that it entered your lungs like a warm soup.

That, of course, assumed that you were breathing through your nose and keeping your mouth shut. If you were dumb enough to walk around with your mouth open after Christmas, the winter air would sear your lungs like a snort of paint thinner and you deserved to die outside like the idiot you were.

The Old Man would be pleased to learn that even respected scientists accept this native wisdom and suggest that little-nosed people are courting disaster if they live north of Birmingham, Alabama.

It is because of The Old Man's vision that I now spend so much of the North Country Winter out on the ice. "I don't know why we do it," Steady repeats in amazement. "We are probably following in a great tradition."

The Old Man bequeathed to me not only his nose but other essential gear as well: tipups, ice skimmer, a gaff, jigging sticks and poles.

I treasure them as I would the relics of a saint, primitive artifacts from a past that never knew the comfort and ease to be found in toasty Sorel boots from Canada, ice augers from Sweden and snowmobile suits that keep you as warm as an igloo.

I fish almost every day of the Winter now, and I think that I love the ice as much as I love the open water. I also think this is what The Old Man must have felt for the North Country in those growing-up years when I thought he wasn't as smart as he turned out to be.

There are great lessons to be learned on the ice, even as there are great lessons to be learned on open water, and I know now what The Old Man was waiting for me to learn up in the Chain of Lakes country. He was waiting for me to be aware.

I don't think he ever used that word or knew it existed, but that's what he was waiting for.

Not just the awareness that the bluegills are schooled at six feet and hitting the green ice fly or that the light tap on the gold Rapala was a bass and not a perch.

It's the awareness that you're sitting out there all alone on the windswept ice like an old Eskimo, removed from the family and waiting for the polar bear to find you.

The awareness that you're sitting out there like a live coal removed from the ring of live coals. Apart. Solitary. Vulnerable. In the mouth of the prowling wind.

Sustained by no others.

Sustained by what, then?

Far out on the ice there are crows settling down on the blinding surface and walking stiffly around the bodies of abandoned dead fish.

One comes eventually to an awareness of the scavengers among us, and one eventually goes beyond the initial revulsion and respects them for what they do in this world.

They go about their work with a ritualistic dignity. They are professional, correct, estimating the logistics of disposing of the dead thing before them. Then they proceed to pick out its eyes.

On the way off the ice this day, I answer the crows and detour a quarter-mile to pick up an empty red Coleman fuel can with which the crows cannot cope.

I call down The Old Man's wrath on the slob who littered. Unless awareness finds him soon, he will be bedridden until Spring.

Something Simple

One of the great beauties of ice-fishing—and there are many—is its simplicity.

You make a hole in the ice and then you sit by it and wait for the fish to find you. Sometimes, when you are running out of patience and body heat, you move around and drill more holes and reset your tipups and perhaps do a little jigging, but in the end, you wind up sitting by a hole waiting for the fish to find you.

"Simplicity," Peter Matthiessen wrote in *The Snow Leopard*, "is the whole secret of well-being."

I was out on the ice the other day, "being simple" as Steady Eddy likes to put it, sitting and waiting and sharing the lake with a dozen other bundled humans, all within hailing distance, none within the range of normal conversation, and so there was no normal conversation.

There was Silence.

Someone coming upon us for the first time could well conclude that some kind of class was being conducted here on the wind-scoured ice, some assembly of students all facing in the same direction, all practicing Something silently, Something that was the ultimate purpose of this frozen Zendo, this monastery without walls, this church without warmth.

What the Tibetan Buddhist calls "crazy wisdom," the non-Tibetan Buddhist is apt to call "crazy stupidity." I think they are both right, because both are the same thing.

It's dumb to sit by that hole in the ice, hour after numbing hour, but when the fish find you, it seems like the smartest thing in the world.

Jigging with an ungloved hand, waiting and watching the hooded, unmoving apparitions as they, too, wait, I had the fleeting flash that perhaps all those snowmobile suits out there were stuffed with Zen monks after all. For, as Peter Matthiessen has so wisely observed: "In keeping with its spare, clear, simple style, in its efforts to avoid religiosity, to encourage free-thinking and doubt, Zen makes bold use of contradiction, humor and irreverence, applauding the monk who burned up the wood altar Buddha to keep warm."

The tipups lay like motionless prayer flags, waiting for wind. Waiting for fish. Waiting for Buddha.

Buddha at the Bottom of the Lake

*I*t happened as it always happens, literally overnight.

One afternoon, the lake is wild with noise and wind. The next morning, the lake is frozen over from shore to shore in the windless silence.

You can't walk on it yet. And it will be weeks before you see the gang out there.

But they'll be here, performing their winter rituals like some exiled priesthood, forsaking the warmth and companionship of the cities, the better to commune with the Buddha at the bottom of the lake.

This ice is their altar and their offerings are green and orange iceflies, live spikes and grubs and fathead minnows, Golden Rapalas and silvery Swedish Pimples.

Today only crows and herring gulls are here, by twos and threes, flying over the newborn ice in their endless quest for things dead—for things dying.

And today, I am here, without thermal underwear, without one of Helen's homemade knit watchcaps that can get you through the Soo Locks in January. My hands are gloveless on the walking stick, my feet in summer boots. I'm just lollygagging and watching my breath at the edge of the glacier.

As I squint at the empty horizon, I see again the squat, bulky figures hunkered down against the swirling snow devils and praying to their gods.

One of the bulky figures, if I'm lucky, will be me. The contemplation of being out there, alone on the ice, brings on an inner glow that is better than brandy.

You watch icefisherfolk closely and they are definitely contemplating something.

"Freezing to death," Steady says, "is one of those things."

One of the other things is the spiritual—especially if you are far from fellow humans, far from shore and far from the schooled walleyes that used to gather below Dave Johnson like pets.

It's the solitude that gets you feeling that you're plugged into a different Area Code altogether. It's the way you felt when you and Charlie Kaiser served Mass at the chapel for the whole convent and you knew that the Seven-Foot Nun was there in the front pew, staring holes in the back of your head and ready to leap right in and pick up the Latin responses the moment you faltered.

One time, when I was serving there alone, my mind went blank right in the middle of the "Confiteor," and the more I tried to remember the worse it became until I got so panicked that I thought of grabbing my side and just keeling over so they would think something catastrophic had seized me, taking not only my Latin, but for the grace of God, almost my young, innocent life.

Never have I felt so mortified, and on top of that I also felt guilty—guilty as sin for doing the devil's own work.

Then the voice of the Seven-Foot Nun boomed in the silence like a great bell, tolling out the Latin phrases she knew better than I knew my own name. Quickly the voices of all the other nuns—there must have been fifty—like daintier, sweeter bells, joined in and I just stared straight ahead. Then it all came back to me and I started mumbling along and pretty soon the nuns' voices got softer and softer and then I was just responding all by myself again.

No one ever said anything about that, except Father Kohler, who told me I wasn't the first server that had happened to and I probably wouldn't be the last. When Charlie found out, he said just the prospect of that happening was enough to make you wet your knickers.

"All true wisdom," Joan Halifax quotes the Caribou Shaman in her book *Shamanic Voices*, "is only to be learned far from the dwellings of men, out in the great solitudes.

"To learn to see, to learn to hear, you must do this—go into the wilderness *alone*. For it is not I who can teach you the ways of the Gods. Such things are learned only in solitude."

When I sit on the ice these days, I hear the "Confiteor" in Latin a lot. Sometimes it's Charlie Kaiser. More often, it's the Seven-Foot Nun.

It's Not the Weather That Frosts You

Steady Eddy figures this would have been a great winter for icefishing if it hadn't been for the weather.

Or, to be specific, if it hadn't been for the way media reports the weather.

"On TV," he laments, "they use words like *bitter* cold, *cruel*, *painful* temperatures and *killer* storms. They make it sound like Siberia out there, so nobody goes out."

The weather has shut down the bait shop for three straight weekends in a row. Weekends are usually bonanzas in normal winters, when the sun is up, the air is calm and the heavy, strong perch coming out of the ice touch your very soul with their vibrations.

Only the hardiest of souls fish when the winds are up, and if the winds are strong even the hardiest of souls stop fishing. The winter winds sweeping the length of North Country lakes have all the sting of the Russian steppe.

The irony is that the winter started out so full of promise. We had ice early. We had snow early. The prognosis was great.

But then, Steady says, the cold settled in, and the media kept reminding everybody that while this particular batch of frigid Arctic air was finally moving out, we had better enjoy the brief respite because an equally frigid batch of Arctic air was about to move in.

"It's not the weather that frosts me," Steady says. "It's the way the media report it. It's enough to scare you out of your Sorels."

Calvin Rutstrum was saying the same thing when he wrote in *Paradise Below Zero*:

> At this writing, in an outer Minneapolis-St. Paul suburb on the St. Croix River, I am looking through an array of picture windows on the heaviest field of drifted snow that has fallen over the Midwest in memory. . . .
>
> Indoors, a battery of thermostats automatically control the desired temperature of each individual room. At hand are the amenities of modern life—good books, stereophonic music, radio, television, and a choice of fine food. Since my body from hours of indoor relaxation has temporarily been deprived of much nerve force and strength, a physically compelling desire obsesses me to remain within the warmth of my shelter.

On the other hand, Rutstrum says, he knows from many winters' experience the value of physical activity in this season, so out he goes into the "frigid atmosphere" to enjoy the durable benefits of a natural winter environment. He goes on:

> I meet the outdoors on its own variable terms. Enjoying an unexplainable lust for the challenge of adverse weather—a sort of love for crisis all through life—I will venture outdoors on foot or on snowshoes with proper

71

clothing no matter how rugged the weather, a blizzard, in truth, being preferred."

The initial effect upon one's comfort, Calvin says, will be apparent: At first, the body suggests—though the mind tends to overrule—that a mistake has been made in even leaving the comfort of indoors at all.

Then, gradually, a change is sensed. The anatomical furnace, having been stoked with food before leaving, starts to generate natural heat—a physiological change from indoor torpor to outdoor animation that becomes surprisingly apparent.

"The Old Guy," Steady says in admiration, "has got that right."

One of the coziest places in all outdoors is an icefishing shack on the windswept ice—and if there's a blizzard blowing, all the better.

Plastic is okay, but we are talking character. We are talking poetry as well as practicality. We are talking what Sigurd Olson in the *Singing Wilderness,* called "the dark house."

Though it was twenty below we took off for the old haunts . . . A tiny tarpaper shack off the end of a long point was our goal. A friend had set it up weeks ago, told us where the spear was cached and the wooden decoy. For its use, we were to bring him a fish. That meant we had to take two. We shoveled the snow away from the door, fanned a flame to life in the little stove, and dug the spear and the decoy out of a drift. Six inches of ice had to be cut out of the hole. We filled the coffeepot, closed the door, and settled down to wait. Outside the wind howled, but the little shelter was cozy and warm. . . .

At first, Sigurd reports, they could see nothing but the green translucent water, but gradually their vision adjusted and they could see farther and farther into the depths, finally to the bottom itself. Liquid streamed through the snow and ice, and the bottom all but glowed.

As the coffee began to simmer, they shed their outer jackets and mitts. Outside, it was still close to twenty below and the snow was whispering. After an hour they began to relax and talk quietly of many things.

If more people had a dark house to fish in, maybe more people would be fishing. Then again, it may not be the weather that spooked people. Maybe it was Steady Eddy himself when he was on National Public Radio's "All Things Considered" with Susan Stamberg the other day discussing ice fishing. When she asked him what a good bait was, he said: "Maggots." When Susan asked him how you kept the maggots from freezing, Steady said: "You keep them in your mouth until you use them."

Steady said Susan freaked out. He also said, "That's eastern folks for you."

BOATS

Of Youth and Wooden Boats

A friend of mine who was raised up in the North Country of long ago just bought himself a wooden guide boat from that era. It's a classic and he means to restore it.

I think he also means to restore a bit of his youth.

"They don't build fishing boats," he laments, "like they used to."

Indeed, they don't. They build them now of aluminum. Or fiberglass. Or plastics. But rarely of wood. Wood is expensive. Requires caulking. Painting. Maintenance. A wooden boat makes as much sense in our plastic society as a wooden airplane.

Yet, I remember the time when the only fishing boats you saw on the northern lakes were wooden boats. They were all handformed, delicately ribbed, beautiful as canoes, with brass fittings to boot. The oars were handcarved too. Those oldtimey boats had as much character as the fishermen—and women—who rowed them and loved them.

Not just the Williamson family on Trout Lake. But George Kennedy over in Minocqua. John Weiss, the Dobbs clan, and the Stanzils on the Three Lakes Chain. Charlie Boy on the Big Arbor Vitae. Doc Olson on the Little Arbor Vitae. Big Porter Dean over in Boulder Junction. And Dynie Mansfield from Little Trout to the Michigan border and beyond.

There were flat bottom boats and round bottom boats and then there were the guide boats, all wooden, all painted green and all serious fishing craft. I spent all of my boyhood in them.

Those were the days when walleyes had to be fifteen inches long to be legal, the bag limit was seven fish and The Old Man would catch both limits while I was learning how. When we heard an outboard motor on the lake, we'd stop and gawk for twenty minutes.

Those were also the days when the anchor was a paint can full of cement tied to about seventy-five-feet of clothesline.

Just now I remember the time on Big Arbor Vitae when The Old Man ordered me to drop the anchor as we drifted in over the gravel bar.

"Deep here," I said as the line raced out over the gunwhale. Then, as if uninvolved, I watched in horror-stricken paralysis as the unsecured end of the line disappeared over the side.

"But," The Old Man said, tapping a finger to his head, "not deep here."

God knows how many wooden boats I not only rowed, but scraped and caulked and painted for The Old Man. The resort always had eight or ten or a dozen around and in the Springtime I hated them all. I cursed them all as I caulked them and I prayed for a maintenance-free boat that would just take care of itself.

My friend who was raised up in the North Country of long ago says he was the same way. And now that he's older, wiser, and pretty well fixed, he has collected a pile of Pfleuger Supreme reels you wouldn't believe. And his first wooden guide boat.

His kids just gawk at him.

Voices of the Dells

We sat on the rock outcropping high above the main channel of the Wisconsin River looking down on the river through the fishnet foliage of leaves and branches, hidden away as hunters in a duckblind.

We could hear the breezes and the birds and the trees talking. We sat silent as stones and listened to the silence.

"It must have been like this when the Indians were here," Marion said in a soft whisper. "Still."

In the very next instant, the stillness was blown away in a bomb-burst of sound.

A barge-like tourist boat was pounding heavily through the startled water stampeding the whitecaps like frightened animals driven insane by fear. They crashed blindly into the rock walls and broke apart and ran wildly together searching for surcease.

Then a metallic woman's voice amplified beyond the human scale raked the canyon like automatic weaponfire and the natural sounds were no more.

"This is called the Narrows," the Terrible Voice proclaimed, "because this is the narrowest part of the river. We are now passing over 150 feet of water. . . ."

I don't know what else the voice said because I shut it out. I wanted to silence that voice and I wanted to cry because the river was helpless and I was helpless.

"That's how the Indians must have felt," Marion said. "Anger. Anger. And sorrow."

Then the boat and the Terrible Voice were gone and still the waters talked in panicky bursts and refused to be gentled.

"It's better for the river at night," Marion said. "The boats are fewer and there is a time to rest."

We moved away from this spot and Marion found the hawk feather, brown splashed on white and delicate as a God's Eye.

"It's either a Cooper's or a red-shouldered," she said. "That's as close as I can get."

Wherever it came from, I knew it was the Indian's sign. And the sign of all those beings who stand on the high shores of this world, screened from sight, watching.

I picked up the packsack and we walked inland.

Always Up Murphy's Creek

You don't expect a canoe trip down Murphy's Creek to be all that memorable because Murphy's Creek is not exactly the Quetico—or, as Steady Eddy likes to put it, "No matter where you are on Murphy's, you are always up the crick."

This trip got memorable in a hurry.

I fell in.

Hugh Percy and Barb and I had a leisurely Sunday breakfast at Mickie's—Madison's earliest Sunday-morning service, Steady calls it—and then we drove over to Wingra to launch the canoe below the dam.

Perce asked if I wanted to "ride or guide," and, since it was his canoe, in the tradition of the *voyageurs* of old, Perce was the *bourgeois*, our trusted leader, and, as such, should sit in the stern. I should sit up front.

Then a funny thing happened on my way to the bow.

With Perce holding the canoe and Barb holding her breath, I put both hands on the gunwales, the left foot on the bank, the right foot over the gunwale.

It is at this precise point in the retelling of this little parable that Steady likes to observe, with his preacher's grin: *You should have gone to church.*

This bank on which my left foot placed not only its weight, but also its trust, was not a solid, safe bank like Randall—it was a slippery, unsafe bank, as befits a muskrat ramble. Muck and marl and greasy skids.

Perce says it was a thing of beauty. Like Steady Eddy in paratroop boots. Or Chevy Chase in street boots. Flat on my back, half-in, half-out of the water, I was impressed by Perce's cool. Steady would have complimented me on the nice slide and called me out. Not Perce.

"Anytime you're ready," he said.

They drove me home, I changed into dry clothes, dry shoes, and went back to try it again.

We boarded without mishap. Barb said she would see us in two hours at the crick mouth if our luck held. She drove off, chuckling. We were under way on what Perce is pleased to call his Annual Murphy's Crick Sewer Run.

In midchannel, you see both shores, both eyesores, trashy with litter, littered with trash, the bottles, the cans, the plastic bits and pieces, the flotsam and jetsam that won't be flushed away because the bowl is stopped up now and overflowing.

"God," Perce said every now and again.

You can get very depressed looking at this, but you have to look. There is a great lesson in looking, looking, looking until the pain, the hurt that comes in through your eyes fills every space in your body, every space in your mind, and the ugly question floats in your consciousness like a Clorox bottle: *What kind of animal does this?*

The answer, also, is not beautiful. *The highest animal, the most developed animal, does this.*

All over Madison this morning, higher animals sat in churches and prayed to God for God-knows-what. For things they needed. For things they thought they needed. For things probably far removed from a Godforsaken, desecrated little creek.

Higher animals. Sitting in church. Higher animals. Sitting in a canoe.

The problem of waste disposal, Calvin Rutstrum noted in *Challenge of the Wilderness*, is that you can't actually "dispose" of anything.

If all the solids, Rutstrum asserts, were separated from the sewage and burned, the resulting gases would soon make breathing impossible on earth. With many rivers in the nation now open sewers, central governments are demanding that some other means be provided for sewage disposal. Where such legislation has been put into effect, some industries have found another way. They drill several thousand feet into the earth and pump their industrial waste and sewage into the clear artesian water system.

"We have polluted," Rutstrum concludes, "the surface water, the air, the earth's upper crust, now we are in the process of polluting the inner earth. All are bound to merge into ultimate catastrophe. Then where?"

As we drifted past the debris, I remembered the words of George Mendoza, who said there was an ugly, narrow side to many fishermen, "but then is this not true of all men?"

He said a good friend was always warning him that time is running away and soon there will be no rivers and streams to fish, so "get to your dreams now before it's too late."

In *Secret Places of Trout Fishermen*, Mendoza admits that he dreams of rivers and poetry and so is an escapist from the mechanical, sunless canyons of life where "politicians and morbid souls concerned only with money and power choke off the young."

"In man's world," states George Mendoza, "injustice is king. Cities are graveyards of dreams, the drawings of children become old and real too soon. Remember how they first appeared—Picasso's cow or Klee's cat thinking of a bird?"

"I still find innocence in rivers," Mendoza insists, "because rivers make their own paths under the gliders of wind and stars. Sometimes I sit close beside a river and listen to it, listen to it all night, until the sound of water rushing over rocks takes me far away."

I close my eyes and listen to the sound of water in Murphy's Crick.

The Blue Canoe

I went into the marshes the other day, and for the first time since last Fall, I had the Blue Canoe with me. No fishing gear. No fishing companion. Just the Blue Canoe. And one paddle.

In the canefield of river willow, the canoe lay like a fish in a woven creel, helpless and out of its element, calculating the distance to life but unable to bridge it.

I pushed the paddle into the muck and leaned into it.

God, I could almost hear Gordie Sussman wincing: *Never use the paddle as a pole—if you need a pole, use a pole.*

The paddle blade came up, creamy with muck and smelling of marsh. Not rank or gross, just smelling of marsh.

Three pushes more and we floated free of the tangle and into open water. I rested the paddle across the gunwales and stayed on my knees.

Daylight in the swamp, you could hear the voices saying. Daylight in the swamp. There was the vision of Deacon Davis, the Arkansas Stump Jumper, announcing dawn to the whole platoon in the tightened tones that sounded like guitar strings, and then throwing back his head and keening: W-a-a-a-y–b-a-c-k–i-n t h e h i i i-l-l-s. . . .

No one had ever said, "Daylight in the swamp" to you before Deacon. All the years you were growing up and The Old Man woke you to go fishing or hunting, he just gripped your ankle as you slept, and pretty soon you wakened gently, and he was always dressed and saying softly: *Time to go.* Now you do the same thing to Vince and he wakes up the very way you did.

The canoe seemed to sniff out the main current and nosed its way into the channel.

It moved past the depths, where, not too many weeks back, the big buck deer had trotted down the snow-covered ice, never seeing you until the last moment.

It moved past the shallows, where, not too many weeks ahead, the spawning carp will thrash and explode, never seeing you at all.

It moved past the pussy willow clump where the catkins clung to the branches like resting caterpillars.

And there, beyond the pussy willows, washed into the shore, was the dead animal.

It seemed big as a beaver, big as a dog. I shuddered as I stared at it, but the shock of seeing it was not as great as the shock of realizing what it was.

Spread-eagled, on its back, bloated almost beyond recognition. It was huge as a hog, yet its claws, its teeth were those of a rodent.

Muskrat, I said out loud. Muskrat, what happened to you?

And slowly, yet of a sudden, it was as if I could hear an answer to my question.

Death happened to me, came the answer. *Look at me closely, paddler. It will also happen to you.*

I shuddered again. Then I just looked. And looked.

"Ma Nature," Steady would smile. "You better take notes. She's gonna ask questions."

There seemed to be a rip, a tear in the muskrat's belly as though something had been working on it, picking on it.

Hugh Percy always insisted that turtles got around to most dead things in the marshes eventually, kind of tidying up so it didn't get to be a cesspool.

"Death enters through the belly," Carlos Castaneda had written in *A Separate Reality*, "it enters right through the gap of will . . ."

He was writing about men, humans, and perhaps that only applied to humans.

"Muskrats or millionaires," Steady insists, "it's all the same. Down here, it's all under Ma's rules."

After all, Steady argues, is the most natural thing in this world to be belly-up in a marsh, or belly-up in a mausoleum?

Every part of nature, Henry David Thoreau observed, teaches that the passing away of one life is the making room for another. In *Walden* he wrote:

> The skeleton which at first excites only a shudder in all mortals, becomes at last not only a pure but a suggestive and pleasing object to science. The more we know of it, the less we associate it with any goblin of our imaginations. The longer we keep it, the less likely it is that any such will come to claim it. We discover that the only spirit which haunts it is a universal intelligence which has created it in harmony with all nature. Science never saw a ghost, nor does it look for any, but it sees everywhere the traces, and it is itself the agent, of a Universal intelligence.

When I left the muskrat, it wasn't a lonely marsh anymore. The Blue Canoe was still empty, but I had company. Henry David. And Ma. And Steady Eddy.

"All the heavies," Steady likes to say.

On the way back, out of a clear blue sky, there was a hawk feather on the water and you could almost hear Augie Derleth.

At the garage, over coffee, Hugh Percy figured the feather probably came from a red-tail. I think he's half right. A red-tail probably dropped it.

But I know where it came from.

The Thompson

Mike and I waded ankle-deep through the field of fresh-
cut timothy, the clover heads awash in the green surf
like so many bluegill bobbers.

We rounded the corner of the barn and there it was. Bottom up. Bleached. Hidden in the high grass almost like a grave.
The Boat. The Wooden Boat. The Thompson.

A gentle wind stirred the clean, sunwashed grass. Like the
uncut hair of graves, the Good Gray Poet had written.

"It's yours if you want it," Mike said. "Give me a hand
and we'll turn it over."

We tipped it delicately, with feeling, and the sunlight
surged like a tidal wave through a scurrying ant colony. The
dead curled skin of old spar varnish flaked off the interior ribs.
The plywood decking had rotted through where moisture had
collected. The transom area had some small punky places where
the cancerous dryrot had gnawed the sleeping boat. We stared
at it for a long time, a scene out of Andrew Wyeth. A scene
out of Mike's youth. A scene out of mine.

"I got it from an old fisherman," Mike said. "It was a good
fishing boat."

I didn't need to read the manufacturer's nameplate to
know how right he was. The Old Man had one of these boats
in another place, another time. It was green and white with a
golden spar varnished interior and it could handle the heaviest
water no matter how far from home we went to fish the Chain
of Lakes. It was so beautiful you could cry. Its nameplate read:
Thompson Brothers, Peshtigo, Wisconsin.

It came to me at that moment that I didn't know what had
happened to The Old Man's Thompson. Where had it gone?
Where had all the wooden boats gone?

Up North, a lot of them had gone for firewood when they
got good and dried out.

Up North too, a lot of the old flat bottoms and round
bottoms got put on the front lawns and filled with dirt and
petunias until they rotted away.

"It's a terrible thing to kill a boat like that," a guide had told me once. "It's not right. A boat doesn't belong in some field."

He thought the proper burial for a boat was what the Chesapeake Bay oystermen did with their work-weary and worn-out bugeyes. They took them up the myriad protected inlets, secured them in a protected, safe anchorage, and gave them over to the winds and the waters.

"It's like saying goodbye to a Loved One," the guide said. "You do it with dignity."

"I think we can save this one," Mike said. "It needs work. A lot of work. Rick Heinzen over at the Freedom Boat Works can give us an idea. He just loves old wooden boats."

I closed my eyes and there was the green and white Thompson slowing for the channel out of Laurel and then stepping up and planing as we raced across Big Stone for home. The smile on The Old Man's face was not to be believed.

Mecum's Canoe

Bob Mecum and I were always going to go canoeing, but we never got around to it.

He had this beautiful Old Town "Trapper" model hung from the rafters in his workshop. It was fifteen feet long, fifty-some pounds, and every time I saw it, I thought of Sigurd Olson up in the Northwest Territories. I also thought of The Old Man and his Thompson out of Peshtigo, because water craft made lovingly, by hand, gets you to thinking that way.

I don't know how often we talked about Bob's canoe over the years, but it was often.

All our family's bikes came from his Monona Bicycle Shoppe—R. C. Mecum & Sons, Family Owned and Operated Since 1961—"Cycling Is Our Only Profession"—and Bob serviced the bikes regularly, from training wheels to ten-speeds.

He did it until his vision deteriorated to the point that he was forced to turn over all the bicycle repairs to his sons, Rob and Tom. To keep active, Bob got into sharpening knives and saws.

I remember him in the workshop, with the canoe hanging in the corner, sharpening my filet knives, hunched over the grindstone, his face only inches from the steel and the flying wheel, his face intense with the unblinking dedication of the Scots clan.

You could picture him in the kilt, the bagpipes crying like banshees above the battle. It's no wonder the Germans called those relentless stalkers "the ladies from hell."

I always flinched when Bob got his face that close, but he never flinched.

Then his eyes went altogether, and in 1978 he spent a month at the Leader Dog School in Rochester, Michigan. When he came back he had Rocky, the gentle yellow labrador, who, as Bob says, "really lacks courage"—but then, as Steady observes, Bob has enough for both of them.

When I stopped in the other day, Bob got to talking about his passion of the last couple of years, ham radio, and how he was getting himself ready to take the code exam soon for his Extra Class license.

"That's the highest license the FCC has for hams," he said. "You have to take twenty words a minute in code."

Since he got on the air in 1979, Bob Mecum has sailed through the first four FCC classes: Novice, Technician, General, Advanced. He has "worked" all the United States, all the continents and seventy-five countries—"which isn't really a lot, considering that there are over 300."

He takes over twenty-five words a minute in code now, but, as always, he is an unblinking realist:

"Sure, I can copy twenty-five reasonably well," he says, "but that's not under pressure. I've got my fingers and toes crossed. And if I don't pass the exam this time, I'll just take it again another time."

Then he mentioned that he wanted to put up a new antenna with a beam and a rotor that he figured would increase his output considerably—"like going from 100 watts to 1000." His present antenna, a vertical, "was not too efficient."

"What I'd like to do," he said, "is convert the canoe into an antenna."

He had never really considered selling the canoe before. As a matter of fact, when the family had a garage sale, a man

had spotted the Old Town hanging in its corner and had offered
$1,500 for it. Bob's wife, Betty, turned down the offer.

"She did right," Bob says. "At that time it wasn't for sale
at any price. I was saving it for Rob and Tom to use."

Rob and Tom have used it only sparingly, and the canoe
hasn't been in the water for the last two years.

They have other interests, Bob says. They not only run
the Bicycle Shoppe along with Betty, they also take classes at
the UW. Tom has a bachelor's from the UW. Rob, who doesn't,
has accumulated 160 credits—enough, according to his advisor,
to qualify him for his master's "when you sit down with this
and work it out."

Bob is proud to boasting of both sons.

"They're not only smart," he says. "They're good with
their hands. They're just not into canoeing, and of course now
I can't see it either."

Bob called for Rob to help, and I held the canoe while
Rob unhooked the chains from the rafters. We lowered it gently
and carried it to a place in front of Bob.

"How does the inside look?" Bob asked.

The inside glistened like soft gold, the ribs like those of
a living animal. I swore they rose and fell as a breathing moved
them.

"I remember what it looked like," Bob said.

"The way of a canoe," Sigurd Olson wrote, "is the way
of the wilderness and of a freedom almost forgotten. It is an
antidote to insecurity, the open door to the waterways of ages
past and a way of life with profound and abiding satisfactions.
When a man is part of his canoe, he is part of all that canoes
have ever known."

I looked into Bob Mecum's eyes, kind now as they were
kind always, eyes that couldn't see me standing three feet away
from him.

We could have been voyageurs staring into the far horizon, searching for landmarks and landfalls, listening for rapids
and watching for wind.

"I can't use the canoe," Bob said, "because I can't see. I
would never get in a canoe again. Of course, if you were to
take it to the Mackenzie River, I would change my mind."

"A blind man, a bohunk and a dog," Steady Eddy said
later, "on the Mackenzie. Northwest Territories. Count me in."

HUNTING THE SILENCE

Looking for Grouse

We spent the other day, my Hunting Friend and I, looking for grouse in the Baraboo Hills.

We didn't see a single grouse, but I did see a whole different side of my Hunting Friend.

"I really can't just go for a walk out here," he said. "I have to take the gun along."

He stood easy, the stock of the shotgun snugged professionally under his armpit, the dog raring to go.

"But," he added, "I really don't care whether I fire it or not."

This day he never did get to fire it, because we never saw a bird. He said he had been out with his brother the week before and they had seen "at least thirty-five birds," and had had good shooting. He also said he was just as happy today as he had been then. Every day he could spend walking the ridges was a special day, and he could have the time of his life just watching and listening and poking around.

There are a lot of guys carrying shotguns around, Steady Eddy insists, who don't want to be mistaken for birdwatchers and nature lovers.

"It's getting tough for me to kill," Mel Ellis told me once for *Wisconsin Trails* magazine and Mel had been a hunter all his life.

"I've got a theory," he said, "that eventually no one will shoot anything or kill anything. It's just a matter of becoming civilized."

Hunting, Mel felt, is a "barbaric throwback." His view is that we've been hunters for tens of thousands of years longer than we've been anything else, and if we don't satisfy this instinct in the actual hunting of game, we satisfy it in the fields of business, or sport, or something like that. His conclusion was that we've been hunters so long we don't know what else to be.

"Someday," Mel prophesied, "we are going to be civilized, but it's going to be another thousand, two thousand, five thousand years. If man is still around then, he's going to be civilized."

Aldo Leopold, writing in *A Sand County Almanac*, thought that hunting—as well as fishing and other outdoor activities, for that matter—depended upon the idea of *trophy*.

The trophy, whether it be a bird's egg, a mess of trout, a basket of mushrooms, the photograph of a bear, the pressed specimen of a wildflower, or a note tucked into the cairn on a mountain peak, is a *certificate*. It attests that its owner has been somewhere and done something—that he has exercised skill, persistence, or discrimination in the age-old feat of overcoming, outwitting or reducing-to-possession. These connotations which attach to the trophy usually far exceed its physical value.

The feather in your cap, Steady Eddy observes, is usually from a pheasant or a partridge, and not from your ordinary chicken.

Just now, I remember Bonnie Connie Jaeger telling me how he hung around the camp more and more during their annual deer hunt, doing the cooking, cleaning the cabin, tidying up, making work, and when he did get out on a stand with his rifle, he didn't even load it anymore.

"You have to take a gun out there," he laughed. "You'd look pretty foolish pointing your finger."

It's probably some kind of evolution going on that we don't understand. Or perhaps we do understand and don't want to admit it.

I think a lot of the Old Hunters are among our most sensitive people—right up there with the birdwatchers and the nature lovers. I have no qualms about having Mel Ellis or Aldo Leopold or Bonnie Connie in charge of things. They are what the poet-naturalist Stephen Levine calls *planet stewards*.

The planet steward, he says, seeks neither death penalty nor hunting trophy. The steward waters the plants and feeds the animals and does not work to waste. For the steward, birdsong and swaying branch are grace; meditation is a step at a time through the wilderness. The steward's way is love, the steward's medium is work, the steward's senses are antennae for necessity.

My Hunting Friend and I followed his dog up and down the ridges. We saw red-tailed hawks and a plump deer, and magnificent clumps of glowing bittersweet.

It was easy to forget we were looking for grouse.

Flusher Pheasant

Walking through the prairie the other day, I flushed the fattest pheasant I'd seen all year, and the bloodrush of my great, good luck felt like standing ankle-deep in champagne.

"With feet like yours," Steady Eddy insists, "you don't need luck to flush birds. You don't even need a dog."

The pheasant was a rooster, big and beautiful as a cargo plane. He lumbered away, wary but not panicked. Noting, probably, that there was no Open Season. No dog. No gun. There was just this hiker with the noisy feet.

And this hiker is harmless.

True, I carry in the pocket of a long lived-in field jacket one solitary .22 caliber long rifle cartridge. The casing is as polished as my rosary beads used to be.

This bullet, I'm sure, must be the only unfired survivor of all the .22 ammunition made that year.

This bullet is all that survives of the years and years I spent in hunting.

Growing up in an industrial city, I didn't come to hunting as naturally as the kids who grew up in the country, but I think I got to love it as much as they did once I got the hang of it.

Getting the hang of it took a little time, because the only place in town The Old Man would let me shoot the .22 was in our basement, below the tavern, and what I shot at was rats.

The basement was poorly lighted, one bare bulb near the ceiling. Gloomy. In the shadows, spooky things lurked. The coal bin. The coal furnace. The root cellar. Cases and cases of beer bottles, full and empty. And rats.

I shot them. The survivors got smarter, and I got smarter, and then I graduated to the woods in Waukesha County.

On my first trip I fired into a squirrel's nest. The Old Man ripped the rifle out of my hands and wrapped it around a tree and said that I was too damn dumb to go hunting just yet.

The Old Man said there were ethics involved in killing things. He didn't use the word "ethics" but that's what he was talking about.

You don't kill all the breeding stock.

You clean and eat and don't waste what you kill.

And you sure as hell don't cause unnecessary suffering or fire a gun into a squirrel's nest.

It all made sense to me then.

Hunting for meat was a noble way of providing.

"Indians are meat hunters," The Old Man would say. "You know better hunters than the Indians?"

Hunting was also a way of growing up, a rite of passage, a touching of the Great Mystery. You learned about death because you brought death.

Perhaps that's why the Indians identified with their kills— as we have never learned to do. Perhaps, too, that's why the Indians believed—as we still don't—that if you kill without a good reason, then you are also a dead thing even though you still walk.

When The Old Man moved to Big Stone Lake, the guns in one cabinet almost outnumbered the fishing rods in another.

We went after deer. Rabbit. Grouse. Partridge. Squirrel. Pheasant.

In the winter, I even put on a white bed sheet and went after crows with a scoped .22.

The crows turned out to be smarter than the rats.

In a way, hunting still makes sense to me, but I don't do any of it anymore.

I really don't know why. It was the most natural thing we did.

I remember my mother knocking down partridge with her .410, each bird so neatly decapitated that The Old Man swore she couldn't have done better with a filet knife. Whenever they bumped into Father Himmelsbach up on those Michigan border backroads, they'd slip him a couple of birds when they saw his gamepocket was empty. They said it was like tithing.

I remember the huge bucks strung up outside the cabin in the Rainy River country, and the good feeling as we went back on the water to fish lake trout in the shadows.

I remember hunting the fringe of the Nicolet National Forest as the snowflakes began to fall and the silence began to deepen, and seeing the deer long before the deer knew I was there. I remember not firing, but I really don't know why.

I looked at that solitary, shiny-nosed .22 cartridge and damned if I know why I haven't dropped it into a deep lake or a shallow trout stream.

The only reason that makes any sense at this late date is that the next time things get tough and dicey and somebody says, "It's time to bite the bullet again," I don't want to come up empty.

Old Man Schweitzer

*T*he season is open in the grouse woods now, the tamaracks are smoky gold and there is that same expectant hush that hangs inside an empty church.

The ambience makes you want to whisper. Any sound seems an act of trespass. In the silence, the birds are hunkered down, waiting for you to make your next move, waiting for you to become so life-threatening that they will make theirs.

Then they will burst from cover, scattering for their lives, almost stopping your heart in the process. It is awesomely difficult hunting because you must be ready at all times, and inevitably, when the birds flush, somehow you are not ready.

"This is written," Aldo Leopold noted in *Sand County Almanac*, "for those luckless ones who have never stood, gun empty and mouth agape, to watch the golden needles come sifting down, while the feathery rocket that knocked them off sails unscathed into the jackpines."

It gets in your blood.

I remember The Old Man, after the doctor told him not to walk the woods anymore, road-hunting all the back roads with my mother, munching their lunches as they drove, the heater and the Wisconsin football game on low, the *slooowwww*, *eeaaaasy* stop when they spotted birds, *eased* out of the car, *eased* the shotguns out of their cases and got their signals straight. That car got to be as good a pointer as most dogs.

They filled up the freezer with birds and I don't think they ever thought twice about their sport or were ever troubled about the killing.

I remember Baba Jula killing chickens with an axe when we were growing up, so the family probably came by it naturally. Killing animals was never a problem.

"Everybody kills something," Steady Eddy is fond of saying. "It could be a deer. Or a trout. Or a rally in the seventh inning."

It got me to thinking about the sainted Dr. Albert Schweitzer, who set up his hospital at Lambarene in the African jungle, and who, it was said, wouldn't kill a fly, let alone a chicken or a ruffed grouse.

Dr. Schweitzer promulgated "Reverence for Life," actually, in the German, *"Ehrfurcht für dem Leben,"* which can be translated into *"Honor and Awe for Life,"* an even heavier trip, Steady argues, than your basic reverence.

"A man is really ethical," the good doctor wrote, "only when he obeys the constraint laid on him to help all life which he is able to succour, and when he goes out of his way to avoid injuring anything living."

Now, can you imagine bringing that up with the bear hunters in Iron County? Or the musky fisherman over breakfast in Boulder Junction? Or Baba Jula with that glint in her eye and that axe in her hand?

"I would," Steady says, "pay money to see it."

A man who is ethical, Dr. Schweitzer explains, does not ask how far this life or that life deserves sympathy, or how far, how much, it is capable of feeling.

To an ethical man, he insists, life is simply sacred. "He shatters no ice crystal that sparkles in the sun, tears no leaf from its tree, breaks off no flowers, and is careful not to crush any insect as he walks. If he works by lamplight on a summer evening, he prefers to keep the window shut and to breathe stifling air rather than see insect after insect fall on his table with singed and sinking wings."

The words get you thinking that Dr. Schweitzer not only lived on another continent, he lived in another world.

The reality, as Wendell Berry puts it, is different in this one. He speaks for everyone who walks the woods these days, without a gun, with a rising anger.

"And now, I find lying in the path," Wendell Berry reports, "an empty beer can. This is the track of the ubiquitous man Friday of all our woods."

In his walks Wendell never fails to discover some sign "someone" has preceded him.

I find his empty shotgun shells, his empty cans and bottles, his sandwich wrappings. In wooded places along roadsides one is apt to find, as well, his overtraveled bedsprings, his outcast refrigerator, and heaps of the imperishable refuse of his modern kitchen.

A year ago, almost in this same place where I have found his beer can, I found a possum that he had shot dead and left lying, in celebration of his manhood. He is the true American pioneer, perfectly at rest in his assumption that he is the first and the last whose inheritance and fate this place will ever be. Going forth, as he may think, to sow, he only broadcasts his effects.

On weekends, too, the hunters come out from the cities to kill for pleasure such game as has been able to survive the constraints and destructions of the human economy, the highway traffic, the poison sprays. They come weighted down with expensive clothes and equipment, all purchased for the sake of a few small deaths in a country they neither know nor care about. We hear their guns and see their cars parked at lane ends and on the roadside.

The reality is also that at Lambarene Dr. Albert Schweitzer did indeed keep a gun. We have his own word on it. His own admission. His own rationale.

He used the gun, he says, "only to shoot snakes and predatory birds."

It just goes to show you, says Steady, that nobody's perfect. Our saints have clay feet, our politicians use pancake makeup, and I've been known to trip over my own snowshoes—when Hugo Willie is carrying them.

HABITATS

Three Lakes

"**Y**ou can't go home again," Thomas Wolfe used to warn us when we were growing up, and we always figured it was because the Greyhound Bus never even had our town on the line.

Of course, as Steady Eddy observes, all you have to do is get the hometown newspaper sent to you and you don't really have to go home at all.

Three Lakes, Wisconsin, isn't exactly my hometown. I wasn't born in Three Lakes. Never went to school there. Never worked there (or many other places, for that matter, as Steady likes to point out to complete strangers), and never did much of the traditional stuff you do in a hometown, unless you count time spent at the American Legion Bar with the locals who call their tobacco chaws *snoose*, their liquor shots *jeets* and game wardens even more exotic names.

Three Lakes is a hometown by adoption, because one memorable day in the misty past, after an official residency that hardly filled a summer, my friends and neighbors decided that I was to be the area's monthly quota for the armed services and if the truth be known I was kind of eager to go, figuring that the sooner I left, the sooner I'd be back, a full-fledged member of that exclusive club that never strayed too far from its home base at the Legion Bar unless it was to take walleyes in the spring, venison in the summer and trout at all times.

I have a soft spot in my psyche for Three Lakes—it's sort of a Lake Woebegon without Norwegians—and a gift subscription to the *Three Lakes News* courtesy of Dear Old Mom, who still knows more dirt than the paper dares print. The News is Dan Satran's sprightly weekly that covers northeastern Oneida County like the spruce budworm. That includes, you understand, not only Three Lakes, but also Hiles, Argonne, Monico, Sugar Camp, and Clearwater Lake. Dan goes on this week:

> You may have read a front page news item about Joe Lassan of Eagle River, age 66, probably drowning or perishing from a heart attack while swimming in the river here.
>
> I first met Joe when we arrived here and he was running the historic Crystal Springs facility [one-time hotel and dining room] at the water's edge just north of downtown Eagle River.
>
> Joe loved the river and the Chain of Lakes and used to run an old, wooden inboard as an excursion boat from Crystal Springs through the Chain.
>
> I rented space in the boathouse from Joe to keep my first boat, and under the boats there, an assortment of fish sought sanctuary—attracted by baitfish and shade.
>
> Joe would lie on the dock, peer under the boats and watch the fish. One day he decided to reach out slowly and see if he could touch a big musky lying next to a moored boat. It slid away slowly, but after a few tries, he could not only touch it, but after a while he could pet the musky.
>
> This may sound like a far-fetched story, but I took a series of photos of Joe stroking his pet musky. It liked the petting so much that like a dog which snuggles up when you rub it under the chin or legs, Joe's pet musky would fin itself upwards until its back actually broke the water's surface as Joe petted the musky.
>
> The photos I took turned out remarkably sharp. We ran them on the front page of this newspaper and the

Milwaukee Journal featured the series in their Sunday sports section.

The publicity about his pet musky led to its downfall. An insensitive fisherman began fishing the boathouse area and caught the musky. Joe was both disgusted and saddened—and so was I.

Joe's health began deteriorating some years ago. He grew a long, mostly white beard and he'd often sit on a bench in front of the old Information Bureau watching the tourists milling around at the corner of Railroad and Wall.

And then I learned he drowned—in the river which was such a big part of his life. The passing of nice guys like Joe is always sad, and I remember him for things like his pet musky and the pleasure he seemed to get introducing the people to the beautiful Chain from his big old boat.

God, and what would you give to be there when Joe Lassan wakes up and there we all are in his big old boat at Crystal Springs and there's this "insensitive fisherman" fishing in the boathouse area for you-know-what and Joe is watching him like an osprey and the fisherman's back is to us and he doesn't see the big old boat drifting down on him and the hands, sensitive enough to pet a musky, are about to pet him?

In *Walden West* August Derleth wrote of another fisherman, John Kleinhein, who lived in a pair of houseboats on the Wisconsin River, moored above the bridge and just over the bank from the railroad station in Upper Sac Prairie:

He was like a symbol left by passing time, a man held over from years of voyageurs and engages, of fur-traders and Indians, of Frenchmen passing down the stream on their way from Quebec, of raftsmen and steamboaters, of dugouts and showboats—one man left to remind those who were growing up in new generations of all time past, all time lost. Yet he had none but a tenuous psychic bond to that past; he did not belong to it except by a thin extension, though his very presence in his houseboat on the river seemed to suggest all that teeming life which had once moved up and down the Wisconsin many decades before. Often by night the smoke of his pipe or cigar drifted up through the darkness, and it stood for a tangible man, the great, fat old man who lived out his years closer to running water, the night and the stars than to anyone in Sac Prairie, one not bowed by misanthropy, but encased in a shell of protective solitude none could pierce. . . .

John Kleinhein and Joe Lassan really lived and died on the same water without ever knowing each other. When you think about it, that's what we all do.

Old Ice House

I think the whole thing started when we were just sitting around on the patio waiting for the bratwurst to cook and listening to the ice cubes clunk and clink in the glasses.

"Ice on a summer's day," Steady Eddy has been heard to say, "is sometimes more welcome than baseball."

Staring down at the rounding cubes in the sun tea, it was easy to dream that they came not from the trays of a General Electric refrigerator but from the January icefields of Big Arbor Vitae.

Once the image of Buckhorn Lodge materialized in my consciousness, I was gone from the patio, poking around in the sawdust-filled icehouses of the past. Not houses made of ice in the winter, but houses made of wood to hold ice in the summer—the windowless structures that preserved the ice that preserved the walleyes that The Old Man pulled out of all the north country lakes that stretched from Pelican in Minnesota to Planting Ground in Wisconsin.

In those times, the winter ice was sawed up and taken from the north country lakes exactly as it had been in Henry David Thoreau's day. Thoreau wrote in *Walden*:

> While yet it is cold January, and the snow and ice are thick and solid, the prudent landlord comes from the village to get ice to cool his summer drink; impressively, even pathetically, wise, to foresee the heat and thirst of July now in January—wearing a thick coat and mittens! It may be that he lays up no treasure in this world which

will cool his summer drink in the next. He cuts and saws the solid pond, unroofs the houses of fishes, and carts off their very element and air, held fast by chains and stakes like corded wood, through the favoring winter air, to wintry cellars to underlie the summer there. It looks like solidified azure, as, far off, it is drawn through the streets. These ice cutters are a merry race, full of jest and sport, and when I went among them they were wont to invite me to saw pit-fashion with them, I standing underneath.

After a while they all merge together and become one icehouse. Buckatabon, Fence, Island, Long, Spider—all those quiet shrines become one building in the very way that all churches become one church and when you enter the soft, filtered hush, it is all the same whether you are in Orly or Dijon or South Milwaukee.

It was a mark of trust when The Old Man finally permitted you to be in charge of the fish icing, to be responsible for burying them in the wedges between the ice blocks—crammed in like climbers fallen into a glacial crevasse, sometimes still tied together on the long stringer so that when you found one later, you found them all.

Even as the walleyes had schooled together in the deep waters of the lake, so they stayed schooled together in the deep ice under the sawdust. You marked their resting places with stakes, in the stillness where the sun never entered. As the summer wore on and The Old Man kept catching his limit of walleyes—seven fish per day, every day of the season—the marker stakes spread and the little cemetery grew as all cemeteries grow wherever man casts his shadow. The silence in the icehouse could be uncanny. It almost rang.

The icehouse gave you your first "hands on" experience, as they like to say now, in burying creatures that you had first encountered while they had life.

Thoreau wrote:

> In the winter of 1846-47 there came a hundred men of Hyperborean extraction swooping down onto our pond one morning, with many carloads of ungainly-looking farming tools—sleds, plows, drill-barrows, turf-knives, spades, saws, rakes and each man was armed with a

double-pointed pike-staff, such as is not described in the New England Farmer or The Cultivator. I did not know whether they had come to sow a crop of winter rye, or some other grain recently introduced from Iceland. As I saw no manure, I judged that they meant to skim the land, as I had done, thinking the soil was deep and had lain fallow long enough. They said that a gentleman farmer, who was behind the scenes, wanted to double his money, which, as I understood, amounted to half a million already; but in order to cover each one of his dollars with another, he took off the only coat, ay, the skin itself, of Walden Pond in the midst of a hard winter.

There is a bass lake west of Eagle River, where, if you watch carefully as you work the lily beds that lie tight to the overgrown shore, you can still see the tumbled remains of an old icehouse, going back into the brush, going back into the ground.

You can't tell what it is from the lake. It's a building that caved in. The first time I cast that shore, I thought it might be an old cabin, because all you could see was the collapsed roof covering everything like a tent.

The undergrowth made it practically unapproachable. You had to tie your boat to fallen trees and wade in. Under the roof, the rotting walls lay without window openings, flattened as if by some behemoth paw. This old house, built by man to hold the Winter inside, had been broken, finally, by the Winter outside. Because at the last, there is no holding that Winter.

There is the same stillness about this icehouse that there was about all the others, and if you clambered down into the tangle and looked, *really looked*, there would be the same stake markers, too. One day I will look for them.

Rock Island

*H*oward Mead, who publishes *Wisconsin Trails*, reminisces in the current issue about one of his favorite places in Wisconsin: Rock Island, 900 timbered acres lying a thousand yards and a thousand years beyond Washington Island in the cold, clear water off Door County.

"My love affair with this beautiful chip of land," Howard writes, "began fifteen years ago when I visited the island with writer George Vukelich and photographer Vern Arendt. We were preparing an article about the place, which was then Wisconsin's newest state park. . . ."

Then he quotes from that article:

> The island is by turns moody and sunlit, somber and serene, very like the men—now long gone and buried— who at one time claimed the land as their own.
>
> A person has to be at peace with himself to appreciate Rock Island . . . for to visit Rock Island is to view, through a small crack, the immensity of eternity.
>
> Rock Island had a powerful effect on me at the time. I don't know if George or Vern have ever been drawn back to the island, but I couldn't stay away. . . .

The very next year, Howard reports, he returned with his family to spend an unforgettable week experiencing the "island feeling"—a sense of aloneness and isolation, a feeling that time itself is suspended. Day by day, the family's usual frantic pace slowed and slowed again. Its scheduled existence switched off as all the familiar sounds of civilization—motors roaring, doors slamming, telephones ringing, and radios blaring—abruptly vanished. In their place was a new sound—the rhythm of waves rising and falling, clicking, swishing on the sand, rolling pebbles together, or striking rock ledges with a thud. It was a new music for the family, and it was ever changing.

You should never go back to a wilderness place, Aldo Leopold insisted. It will not be the same.

I think that's why I never went back to Rock Island.

It wasn't a primeval, virginal wilderness. The earliest human settlements in Wisconsin were here, and current archeological digs suggest the early explorers from the Old World touched these beaches on their way to the mainland.

The Potawatomi Indians were here first, and it is said that some are buried in the ravine below the lighthouse bearing their name.

Legend has it that one of the earliest settlers was David Kennison, the last survivor of the original twenty-four troublemakers who staged the Boston Tea Party in 1773. The story is that Kennison was 110 years old when he and his son lived on Rock Island in a fishing village. Kennison had four wives and twenty-two children, and for a while it looked like he might outlive everybody. He died in Chicago at the age of 116 and is buried in Lincoln Park, his grave marker a granite boulder with a bronze tablet.

One of Rock Island's earliest settlers, a John Boon, lies buried in the island's tiny cemetery along with two of his sons. It is said that John was the brother of the famed Daniel Boone.

And next to John Boon, they buried the ashes of Chester H. Thordarson.

Thordarson was the millionaire genius—"the electrical wizard of Chicago"—who bought 770 of the island's acres in 1910 (the remainder was owned by the federal government and administered by the Coast Guard) and who left his mark upon this island as no other human has.

"The tracks of the others," I wrote fifteen years ago, "have been obscured by the wind and the seasons and the long years. . . . Perhaps they were then, as we are now, inconspicuous in life with no grand dream to dam the flow of eternity. Thordarson was different. He had a grand dream. . . ."

At the height of the Depression, he built his famous stone boathouse and great hall at a rumored cost of $300,000. The impressive structure, which stands stolidly today, was in the style of Althing, Iceland's parliament building. In this great hall, Thordarson installed a priceless 25,000-volume library containing rare scientific and Icelandic texts. The collection was eventually purchased by the University of Wisconsin for a quarter million dollars.

What I remember most vividly is the meandering remains of a stone fence bisecting the island. On this, cedar posts strung with hog wire were once implanted to keep the island's white-tailed deer away from the exotic seedlings and plantings that Thordarson was trying to establish in formal gardens.

I think Chester Thordarson truly loved nature, loved his island, and his fence was an attempt at coexistence. When the fence failed to keep the deer out, he had great deer drives organized, and the locals from Washington Island were permitted to hunt them. When I saw the island, the exotic gardens were long gone, and from the signs, the deer were thriving.

Perhaps the lesson was: *To love something is not necessarily to possess it. And to possess something is not necessarily to be loved by it.*

If I could speak to Thordarson, I wrote once, I would like him to know simply this: Old Man, we have been to your island. There are others coming. To walk the wild beaches. To view the great dark gulls over the timeless reefs. To spend a quiet moment at your grave and tell you how it is with us.

Your markings are here, kept with honor.

We who come now take nothing away from Rock Island. Not a stone. Not a flower. Not a single, solitary dimensional thing. And yet, what we can take away from Rock Island can never be taken away from us.

That's why I don't go back to Rock Island. I never really left it.

Hugo Willie's Gasoline Emporium

A walk through the Arboretum is just never complete unless you can stop off at Hugo Willie's Gasoline Emporium on the way home. The emporium is owned, operated, and kept out of bankruptcy by Hugh Percy—Perce to his wife, Hugo Willie to his friends, and Mister Hugh Percy to the real world.

There it sits on the fringe of suburbia—a little way station on the highway of life, a haven for the weary walker, a place to take the load off your feet and the road off your mind.

It's like one of those Yukon cabins in the old days where the door was always left unlatched, the essentials for survival stored dry inside, freely offered to anyone who dropped in and needed them, with the understanding that you would use only what you absolutely required for survival, leaving something for the next wanderer and maybe replacing the stove wood.

107

It's like that here, only in this cabin Hugo Percy greets you with a cup of coffee, solicitous of your comfort and calluses, exchanging the news of the day, weather shifts, and the sightings of hawks.

It's old-timey like Hugo Schwenker's harness shop used to be in Sauk City, and Bill Boelter's Texaco and Bait Station way, way up in Woodruff. Way stations, indeed.

In October, Perce thought he was going to lose his station because a veterinarian wanted to buy it and put in a pet clinic. That was okay with Perce's landlord if the zoning could be changed from residential to commercial.

All his friends—well, a lot of them—also thought Perce might lose his station.

We had been with him when he was on Speedway—Mineral Point Road across from Glenway Golf Course. A couple of service bays there justified the presence of Jerry and Bill on the roster, first-rate mechanics who knew as much about your car as they knew about the coho running off Racine or the walleyes off Weyauwega. The whole crew cooked out a lot at this location, and sometimes you got the feeling that it wasn't so much a service station as it was a deer camp after the morning drive. Sometimes when they yelled at Rudy Ploc across the road as he started up the balky foursomes, you got the giggly sense that the old Hard Rock might just fire a shot across the bow for effect.

Perce lost that location, and there's a Starvin' Marvin there now. Nothing against Marvin, but no way does that replace Hugo Willie's Gasoline Emporium.

It's like knocking down Mapleside and putting up a hamburger franchise. Or filling in a Monona marsh and calling it Law Park.

Or filling in a Mendota marsh and calling it Lot 60.

"Life," philosophizes Steady Eddy, "is what happens to you while you're waiting for the bulldozers."

His customers stuck with Perce the way the wagon train stuck with Kit Carson as he led them through the sea of prairie grass.

When Perce found the tiny blue-roofed hut at 3600 Monroe we followed along to the oasis, rejoicing in the friendly sparrows living on the roof and the even friendlier folks living next door and all around.

Steady Eddy found Perce's on the city map and approved.
"It'll make a nice rest stop," he told me. "God knows,
you stop anywhere in Nakoma and you're gone."

The station had only one peewee service bay, which works
out well for one peewee car. Steady says the whole operation
was probably designed by Honda and will undoubtedly be fran-
chised soon.

"The average car will fit in most stations," he says. "This
station will fit in your average car."

With only that one service bay, Hugo Willie's became, of
necessity, a one-person operation. There just wasn't any physical space for Jerry and Bill to work on cars.

They keep in touch, though, stopping in regularly, and I
wish Rudy Ploc was here to see them, chattering animatedly
about the big chinook from the big lake—some "roostered"—
lost, some "in the box"—not lost—as they stand around the
cast-iron stove that Perce picked up and cleaned and hasn't
gotten around to connecting up yet.

Of course, Rudy would be quick to observe, if you hooked
up the stove you couldn't lean the snowshoes against it anymore. And with so much hot air generated in one place you
don't really need to be creating more, you need to be circu-
lating what you've got before it all collects up at the ceiling
and overheats the sparrows living in the attic.

It was Perce's friends and neighbors who saved the little
birdhouse of a service station.

We watched them all on cable TV one night, testifying
for the station to continue, as is. Albeit untidy—a little—but
who wants to have your car looked after in a place where the
birds are on tape and they don't have real beaver cuttings in
the display windows?

The veterinarian testified, too.

Alderperson Jean Stewart said she supported the Plan
Commission's recommendation not to rezone and the city
council so voted, which meant that the vet was out and Hugh
Percy was still in.

"With neighbors who grow tomatoes in the front yard,"
Steady says, "how can you lose?"

Hugo Percy, still unperturbed as a falcon, undisturbed as
a Brule pool, fixes you with those startling blue eyes.

"God," he says, "what a beautiful day."
On the roof, the sparrows sang like they did for Assisi.

The Cabin

Sigurd Olson always said that it took at least three days to get used to the wilderness after you had been in the city a while.

Of course, he was talking about the big woods of Canada and not the little woods of Wisconsin, but he said it held true whether you were up in the mountains or down in the marshes.

Sigurd said you need at least three days to get all the Twentieth Century sound out of your head: the telephones, the radios, the televisions, the computers, the sirens, the horns, the squealing tires. Not to mention the big whizzing cars that gobble up all of the gas and the little whizzing pumps that gobble up all the money.

We have been at the cabin for four days now and if I never knew it before, I know it now. Sigurd Olson was right.

The first three days were winding-down days, Sigurd always said. Head-emptying days. I recall, too, Izaak Walton, that *Compleat Angler*, urging us Incompleat ones: "Study to be quiet."

So our first three days were studying days.

We studied the loons that fish this lake more efficiently than any human angler. They cruise, barely moving on the surface, and then submerge to fish, resurfacing after having covered an impressive distance underwater.

Loons love the water, it seems, more than they love the air. It is rare to see them airborne. When they fly, they're either on their way from fishing or on their way to fishing.

They float along, relax, talk a little and fish an awful lot.

"Any bird," I can hear Steady Eddy saying, "that fishes from dawn to dusk is one smart bird."

This morning as I write this, a solitary loon is fishing the lake while no one else is and I know Steady is right.

Little Brown Bats

*T*he *scritch-scratching* you hear in the cabin's walls comes from the Little Brown Bats that live under the cedar shakes. All day long, they rest there with mewling little movements, packed in like sleeping night workers hidden away from the daytime world in a regular Bat Condo.

The first time you hear them *scritch-scratching* in the shakes can be a little unnerving, because it sounds like they're coming right through the wall.

But then you realize that they're not coming right through the wall and that they have as much right to be there as the shy little garter snake that suns itself next to the coiled, soft garden hose. Or the chickadees picking at the sunflower seeds from the mouth of the Mason jar feeder. Or the chipmunks inside the Mason jar, stuffing their faces with seeds, their cheek pouches bulging like a lawyer's briefcase.

Or *you*, sitting inside the cabin with a cup of coffee and sniffing the clean breeze through the screens, winey with sun-warmed pine and berry bushes.

Between eight twenty-five and eight thirty-five in the evening, the bats come streaking out of their hideaways, low and fast to avoid any waiting owls, and head for a night's hunting of mosquitoes. I think I didn't really appreciate the bats until I cleaned fish one evening, a big pailful of bluegills, and the cleaning took me past sundown and into darkness.

Practically naked except for the cut-off jeans, I made the greatest discovery since Steady Eddy found Cleveland's Lunch: *There were no mosquitoes!*

Now, every cabin between here and Hudson's Bay has mosquitoes, but not this one. Ma Nature and her Little Brown Bats. It was like having Pappy Boyington and the Black Sheep Squadron, flying fighter cover overhead.

Naturalist Ronald Rood, in his book *Animals Nobody Loves*, remembers a night he was showing slides at a children's camp, and because the evening was warm, the windows were open and moths and other insects were swirling around the bright screen. Suddenly, a pair of Little Brown Bats flew in, completely silent except for an occasional chirp.

111

"I took the slide from the projector," Rood relates, "leaving a blank, brilliantly lit screen. As three hundred enthralled children watched, the bats darted in and out of the light. Probably they had followed a moth or two through the window and stumbled across the bonanza near the screen. One after another, the insects had disappeared. Finally, after they had cleaned house, the bats vanished as they had come."

I know one city person who thought it was dumb to use cedar shakes on the roof and bring on the bats, but you have to feel sorry for a person like that.

"That is the kind of person who would put a Pink Flamingo statue in the front yard," Steady would say, "and Pink Flamingo statues eat no bugs."

We studied the full moon from the dock last night as a mist rose from the shore and the lighted cabin on the high bank floated ghostly as an anchored ship. There was no one on the lake, not even the loon.

Off to our left in the little bay, a bullfrog started broadcasting loudly in a series of four bellows. To our right, a lesser bullfrog, a lightweight, answered in a monosyllabic, respectful tone.

After a brief exchange of credentials, the night was still.

There was only the pine-fringed lake, the Big Dipper, and the Deep Sky bigger than our little world.

I thought of all the nights in all the places in Sigurd Olson's wilderness. The Chain of Lakes, Little Trout. The Old Man's haunts. Dynie's.

The Dipper was still here. And the lake. And the bats. But the rest of the Twentieth Century was gone.

It was then I realized I hadn't felt so good, so peaceful for a full year. "Tomorrow," I told myself. "Tomorrow. You join the other loons and start fishing in earnest."

As Steady says, it's the loons of this world who have really got it together.

Devil's Lake

I had a date to go canoeing with our daughter Martha the other morning, but because my back was still a little out of whack, I begged off and we just went for a walk instead.

It wasn't any old ordinary kind of walk either.

We walked a Canadian beach the other morning and got back home in time for lunch.

The rugged, rock-faced bluffs towered above the lake on all sides but the north, the talus slopes sprawling down to the shoreline like some stone glacier.

To the west, the whole beach stretched empty and abandoned.

To the south, the whole lake stretched empty and abandoned.

Offshore, a single gull hung low above the whitecaps, searching out the wave troughs.

In the summertime, thousands of people pack themselves into this North Beach of Devil's Lake. Today, there were just two of us: Marty and her old man.

We walked without talking at first. Along the water's edge. Tasting the scented southwind. Hearing the gulls offshore. Hearing the chickadees inland.

As we walked, I told her how The Old Man had brought us to this very beach a full forty years ago. It had seemed like the wilds of Canada then. Now, on this morning, it seemed like them more than ever.

I told her how Jimmy White and Don and I used to fish the eastern shore for trout. All night long, with gas lanterns hung out over the gunwhales and great trout swirling out of the darkness. In the mornings, we would fish the western shore with flyrods, take fifty fat bluegills apiece, and finally call it a night.

I told her how Russ and Bob and I used to fish the lake in winter, driving onto the ice from the south shore, the expansion cracks booming and racing alongside until your mind played tricks and you felt a little panicky.

I told her how legend had it that Devil's Lake was bottomless and Russ always insisted that a boat sunk in Devil's later turned up in Mendota via an underground river.

She didn't say anything and I could have gone on until sundown because this place is peopled with a lot of ghosts and if I close my eyes I can see them waving, and if I close my ears, I can hear them laughing.

You really should close your mouth now, I told myself. *You should really shut up because all this is probably boring as hell.*

113

Marty just took my hand and smiled that most beautiful of smiles.

"I'm glad we didn't get to go canoeing," she said. "For today, this was much better."

Later, as Marty guided the Honda around the South Shore Drive, I wondered where they all were now: Jimmy White; And Russ; And The Old Man. I think, maybe I know. And then, I think, maybe I don't know anything at all.

"Only the mountain," Aldo Leopold once wrote, "has lived long enough to listen objectively to the howl of a wolf."

Across the haunted lake, the talus slopes waited in repose.

The Concrete Glacier

*B*ob Resch and I were driving south on I-94 in the Wisconsin dawn, heading for the Racine harbor, passing through miles and miles of the commercial and residential sprawl that surrounds the Greater Milwaukee complex.

It felt, suddenly, as it always feels these days, like an alien country. A strange and hostile place. A land under siege.

The gargantuan high-tension wire towers marched across the landscape, a relentless, invincible, invading army, dwarfing everything in the human scale.

The howling columns of trailer-trucks moved like mammoth frenzied animals caught up in some terrifying stampede.

The endless fingers of stone and steel reached everywhere, crusting over everything in a glacier of concrete.

Loren Eiseley was in the bullseye when he called us "The World Eaters."

That's what we are doing. We are eating the natural world and like sightless worms boring through the soil, we too are leaving castings in our wake. But our castings are not easily recycled. They are not easily digested by earth. They are mostly plastic.

A long time ago, Ernest Hemingway wrote in *Green Hills of Africa*:

A continent ages quickly once we come. The natives live in harmony with it. But the foreigner destroys, cuts

114

down the trees, drains the water, so that the water supply is altered and in a short time the soil, once the sod is turned under, is cropped out and, next, it starts to blow away as it has blown away in every old country and as I had seen it start to blow away in Canada. The earth gets tired of being exploited. A country wears out quickly unless man puts back into it all his residue and that of his beasts. When he quits using beasts and uses machines, the earth defeats him quickly. The machine can't reproduce, nor does it fertilize the soil, and it eats what he cannot raise. A country was made to be as we found it. We are the intruders and after we are dead we may have ruined it but it will still be there and we don't know what the next changes are. I suppose they all end up like Mongolia.

We were driving along the fringes of West Allis now.

I was seven years old when we moved here to live on 69th and Greenfield, and The Old Man would take me fishing out to the surrounding lakes: Pewaukee, Tichigan and what he felt was the treacherous Wind. Also Big Muskego. Little Muskego. And even Lake Denoon.

We always fished Pewaukee for the big dark bluegills in forty foot of water with hand-lines. We would fish them off the bottom using hellgrammites, keeping the bait moving by raising and lowering our forearms with a lot of wrist action.

Then we brought them up, hand over hand, just like cod fishermen.

For hours on end in those hazy, muggy Wisconsin days, I would pretend that I was a young doryman on the Grand Banks, but I never told The Old Man.

What I particularly remember about all those auto trips back then was how quickly we were out of the city and into the countryside and how all the farmers worked their fields not with tractors and machines, but with teams of horses.

When we did see a tractor, The Old Man would slow down and we'd gawk a little. I can even remember The Old Man making the same observation about fertilizer that Hemingway made later, and Hemingway turned out to be a lot more circumspect.

The suburbs were sailing past now, flying polaroid prints: Picture windows and tubular swimming pools. Barbeque grills and flashy ski-boats cradled in substantial trailers.

And all the expensive little cars named after animals that are on the very brink of extinction.

I asked Resch if he could live here and he said, well, there were worse places. Tokyo, for one. He also said that Madison wasn't this bad yet, but it was "almost getting there."

And then we were driving along the fringes of South Milwaukee.

It was here that I was born and raised, in what is now called an extended family.

My Grandfather Vincent and my Grandmother Jula are both buried here in one of the little green patches the glacier hasn't reached yet, and the memories rise from the past like startled birds from their roosting tree.

Tata Vincent could place a pinch of soil on his tongue and taste it and tell you what it needed to grow things.

Baba Jula would slit the throats of two white chickens every Easter season, catch their blood in a cup, and mark crosses in red over all the doorways in the house to ward off the evil spirits. Until I got to high school, I thought everybody did that.

Tata, Tata. Baba, Baba. The boyhood words come flooding back through a thin, thin crack in the long-locked door of memory.

I think we are not supposed to open that door. I think we are not supposed to want them back or call them back or hold them here in any way.

There are too many machines in this place. The horses are all gone. The toilets are all inside. What would they do here?

But Tata. Baba. What will our children do now that our soil is sour and our land is possessed by the evil spirits?

Where are we going, I kept asking myself over and over. *Where in the hell are we going?* And where are we taking the Americanized descendants of all the Tatas and the Babas of this world?

It wasn't exactly an omen from heaven, but a partial answer came flashing by on the very next road sign we passed.

Racine, the road sign said. *Racine, Wisconsin.*

Aldo Leopold's Shack

We went to visit Aldo Leopold's shack the other day because Marion Moran couldn't believe I had never visited it.

Marion is a grandmother in chino pants who is regarded by many people as the finest naturalist-teacher now working in our state. Much of her reputation is based on her widely acclaimed "Walks on the Wild Side," the strikingly creative series that she conducted throughout the state for University of Wisconsin-Extension.

I don't think "strikingly creative" is overstating it.

There aren't too many teachers around who have you pressing an ear up against birch trunks and *listening to trees.*

Or who have you hunkering down in the middle of a deep night in a deep woods, listening to the words of Chief Seattle, the Taos Pueblo and the early people who loved this land as few of the later people have.

Marion was going to be taking a class to the Leopold shack, and first, as is her custom, she would be "preflighting" it: walking the trails, checking for "mud and moisture," noting the game trails, the advance of the season, the places most appropriate for seeing birds, or hearing Indians.

So we went to experience what Aldo Leopold called his family's "refuge from too much modernity: 'the shack.'"

"On this sand farm in Wisconsin," Aldo wrote, "first worn out and then abandoned by our bigger-and-better society, we try to rebuild, with shovel and axe, what we are losing elsewhere. It is here that we seek—and still find—our meat from God."

First, we visited with Nina Leopold Bradley, who, with her husband Charles, lives only a short winding walk from the old shed that her father made world-famous.

"In all the photographs," Charles said, "over all the years, the shack is always the same. It doesn't seem to change. But in the background, Nature has changed everything, is always changing everything."

For the Tamarack Press edition of *Sand County Almanac,* Nina Leopold Bradley had recalled that wintry February day

in 1935 when her father hauled the family out to share the joy
of his new purchase: eighty acres (at eight dollars an acre) and
a tumbledown shed filled with frozen cow manure and chicken
droppings. She wrote:

> What did my father see in this place, his daughter
> asked, that put the sparkle in his eyes?
> Did Aldo Leopold truly visualize the deep pine-and-
> oak forest that now, forty years later, shelters deer and
> provides drumming logs for grouse? Did he visualize the
> lush native prairie with its big bluestem grass as high as
> I can reach, its myriad flowers blooming in succession from
> spring to autumn? Did he see the return of the sandhill
> cranes that now dance in the big marsh? Did he anticipate
> the battle now being waged to prevent the aspen and dog-
> wood he planted from taking over his prairie and marsh?
> Did he see a family that would never again view land
> casually?

Nina gave us the key to the shack and said we were welcome to start a fire in the fireplace. That seemed a practical
idea, because the day was turning gray and blowy, the kind of
day ducks come in low and skittering, and the whole marshland
seems to be drifting and moving.

Marion took the binoculars.

I carried the packsack with our lunch.

Once in the woods, there was less wind. The trail was wet
with standing water in the low spots. I was struck by the number of dead trees, standing and unchopped, the oblong holes
of pileated woodpeckers high and prominent, bright in the
grayness.

"They make holes that shape," Marion said, "when they're
feeding. Where they nest, the holes are round."

I know folks who, if they owned this land, would have
long since had the chain saws out and there wouldn't be any
dead trees. There also wouldn't be any live pileateds.

"We abuse land because we regard it as a commodity
belonging to us. When we see land as a community to which
we belong, we may begin to use it with love and respect. There
is no other way for land to survive the impact of mechanized
man. . . ."

It was hard to tell there had been a farm here at all.

Nature, as Charlie Bradley had said, had changed everything. And that was precisely why everything seemed so wild and unchanged. The land had gone back—not to what it had been, but to something akin to what it had been. Something wild. Something unmechanized.

Aldo Leopold was not here, and yet, as we neared the shack, his presence was very much here. I almost felt we were going to encounter him around the next turn.

We encountered, in his place, a huge red-tailed hawk, rising lazily from the edge of a clearing where all wise hunters sit.

We encountered, in his place, three plump deer, their white tails flying, their movement without sound or fear.

The highest use of wilderness, Aldo Leopold once said, is to simply: *Let it be.*

We unlocked the shack, got a good fire going to take the chill off, and ate our lunch. I didn't get the feeling Aldo was inside, watching the fire. I got the feeling he was outside, watching the sky.

Lake Michigan Beach

*E*ver since I was a little boy, I have loved to walk the Lake Michigan beaches.

They are magical zones, these land's end places, where sometimes the birds are silent and the very stones speak. Beaches change overnight. One day clean as a trout's belly. The next, littered with seawrack and seaweed and dead fish, pieces of nets and gear. And anchor chain so heavy no mortal could move it an inch, yet these waters moved it for miles and miles.

Vince and I walked a Door County beach the other day homeward from fishing, the sandpipers scurrying before us like a flock of chickens, the gulls patrolling the shallows for dead things, the great inland sea crashing into rock and land and muttering to itself like an old person, preoccupied. Preoccupied.

119

I watched Vince move down the shore and I knew that young people belong on beaches. They are more amphibian, more flowing, closer to their own creation than we old ones who forget or deny that we are of the water and the water is of us. The young ones do not deny. The pulse of the sea is strong in their souls and they race along the edge of our world happy as otters, serious as clams.

When I caught up to Vince, he was waiting, standing over the dead brown trout, a salmon-sized corpse swathed in the whitish fungus, stretched in the sand like a cadaver posted for autopsy, one eye neatly removed, as if with a scalpel.

Vince knew a gull had taken the eye. He knew a gull would come to take the other.

We moved down the beach and he kept looking back. Looking for that gull. I did not look back. Then he became an otter again and moved away. When I caught up, he was standing over a butterfly, alive but bedraggled with dampness. It lay in the wind, helpless as a capsized sailboat.

Vince got the butterfly on his finger, carried it to a half-buried log, smoothed out the sand on the lee side and placed the butterfly out of the wind, in the hot sun.

He knew it would dry there. He knew too that he felt something for that butterfly. He wished it well, and I remembered how he talked to tulip bulbs when he planted them years ago. Then he was off and away.

I thought about what T'ien T'ung-Hsu had written back in the Eighth Century A.D.

> Nature may be compared to a vast ocean. Thousands of millions of changes are taking place in it. Crocodiles and fish are essentially of the same substance as the water in which they live. Man is crowded together with the myriad other things in the Great Changingness, and his nature is one with that of all other natural things. Knowing that I am of the same nature as all other natural things, I know that there is really no separate self, no separate personality, no absolute death and no absolute life.

Halfway home, we came upon a seagull that did not rise and flee at our approach. It sat high on the beach, legs tucked in, wings tucked in. It seemed unmarked. It was having great trouble breathing. It seemed resigned. It seemed prepared.

We crouched and talked to the seagull and to each other. Vince asked if there was anything we could do and I told him I didn't think so.

I remembered a lifetime ago when we found a dog hidden away in the thick bushes and we kept dragging it out and the dog kept crawling back in. One of the Old Grandfathers told us finally that the dog knew what it was doing and to let it die in peace.

We walked away and kept looking back until we could no longer make out the gull. Then we looked straight ahead.

The Sturgeon Bay Ship Canal

We spent the weekend at the cabin on the beach just south of the Sturgeon Bay Ship Canal. The foghorn sounded every day and every night we were there and I can still hear it, reverberating through my inner space like some great, nameless animal moaning in a darkened cave.

Two moans within a five-second space, then an uneasy silence for twenty-three seconds, then the pair of moanings again and then the silence, throughout the day, throughout the night. Throughout our fitful dreams. Throughout our fitful lives.

In the darkness, we sat on our piece of secure, rockbound coast and listened to the eternal sound, melancholy, but not frightening. We waited for the foil-wrapped potatoes in the driftwood coals. We waited for the fish to be done. We waited without fear.

Jo and Vince and I sat on the log a pebble throw from the restless alien world and I told them of the dark, stormy nights on the ore carriers, the foghorns washed away on the screaming winds, the seas crashing over the cargo holds, the stern lifted high out of the water, the screw spinning, chattering in mid-air, the ship struggling like a drowning animal, fighting, fighting. In those nights nothing was secure, nothing was rockbound and fear pecked at our spirits the way gulls peck out the eyes of dying fish.

Anyone who has sailed the Great Lakes in the great ships can talk to you of fear. Fear of the November storms on the open lakes. Fear of the holy, mystical powers in these living waters. Fear of the alien world.

A lot of sailors will not put these things into words for you, let alone put the words on paper, but I think they would agree with Mike Link, who did put some of these things on paper in the book, *Journeys to Door County.*

"This land," he writes, "should be saved for the sullen, gray foggy days or the blustery, stormy days." He tells of visiting Cave Point with his wife on a thick, foggy day—one that makes you think of London or Maine and foghorns in the gloom.

They were there alone. Billows of damp air rolled in instead of big waves and the water surged, gurgled, and disappeared at the rock's edge. The fog hid the rest of the world and the rocks were wet and seemed to glisten in an otherwise muted scene.

"My thoughts of that day were mixed," Mike Link remembers. "The fog made us seem alone in the world, and the surrealistic setting made my wife's image stand out from a gray background. There was a haunting spell in the air. The fog was not just Lake Michigan water suspended in the sky. There were spirits floating there. Seamen of the fresh water that had tested their mettle in the Great Lakes' storms and had lost. I could feel them."

We stared at the shrouded sea and for a moment, I was back on the fishtug *Ione* out of Two Rivers, watching the LeClair brothers gilling and gutting a ton of laketrout, the waters sparkling and filled with fish and gulls and the laughter of young men who knew damn well they were all going to live forever.

MA NATURE
BATS LAST

Trout Killer

"**M**a Nature bats last," Sleepy Ed used to say up in the Chain of Lakes country, "and she's a pretty tough out."

Sleepy would say this when an October squall was blowing us right off the Big Stone Lake and into Otto's Bar. Or a sudden thunderstorm was hot-wiring the whole of Oneida County and we were caught out in the open water. Or the bottom dropped out of a winter afternoon when the sun seemed to set at three o'clock and the naked trigger finger couldn't find its way back into the shooting mitt.

I think he even said it when the Old Settlers died and we went to see them, combed and clean shaven like they were just dozing in their brand new suits.

I was reading the current issue of *Trout* and I thought of Sleepy Ed and how right he was.

The magazine contains an article titled: "Acid Rain: Trout Fishing's Greatest Threat?" The gist of it is that for the last thirty years, the acidity of rain and snow in the United States has been increasing, corresponding with heavier emissions of sulfur and nitrogen gases in the same period from a heavy national use of coal, oil and gas.

The exhausts from our automobiles and factory stacks rise into the world's wind systems and are deposited miles away, even in remote wilderness areas. Many of these areas are characterized by hard, granite bedrock with thin soils and little buffering capacity, so they cannot completely assimilate or neutralize the acid coming in.

How does that affect the fish?

In the *Trout* article, Dr. Carl Schofield of Cornell University, one of the world's foremost authorities on acid precipitation, puts it this way:

> Normally, we would expect uncontaminated precipitation—relatively pure precipitation—to have pH values that are around 5.7. But now, where we have contamination from strong acids like sulphuric and nitric acids, pH values are 4.0 or less. In sensitive areas like the Adirondack region of New York State, northern New England and perhaps some areas of the Appalachians, when streams and lakes are acidified to pH levels below 5.0, we can expect serious effects upon the fish populations. High mortality and extinction of fish populations have already occurred in many of these acidified areas.

> Can the area affected by acid precipitation be expected to spread?

> It already has to the north where there are now problems in Southeastern Ontario, Quebec and parts of the Maritime Provinces. Expansion to the Western United States is dependent upon power development. Air flow in the U.S. is toward the East and currently most of the strong sources of sulfur from fossil fuel combustion are in the industrialized regions in the East and Midwest. There is some concern for areas in Northern Michigan, Minnesota and Wisconsin that are particularly sensitive, such as the Boundary Waters Canoe Area. As for the far West, there are sensitive regions there in Oregon and Washington and parts of the Rockies and Sierras.

I can just hear Sleepy Ed up at Otto's bar laying out the parameters of our dilemma. It's like multiple choice. Maybe Ma doesn't want us to use fossil fuels. Or nuclear energy. Maybe the whole game is rigged and wired and the answer is *None of the Above.*

Good God, I would tell him.

Now you're talking, he would tell me.

And outside, no human could survive on Big Stone today.

The Healing Alfalfa

Professor Harold "Bud" Jordahl and I fished his farm the other day up in Richland County.

It's not really good farming country, the land is steep: not mountains, but foothills. The hills huddle over the little valleys, high and implacable as elephant rumps. The lower slopes have been row-cropped and badly used for almost one hundred years until now the face of the old land looks like the face of an old woman, tired and seamed and sucked of life.

But there is life here.

Nature is working quietly to revive this place, and because of my professor-friend and his smarts, Nature's work is a little easier now than it used to be here.

Bud has a thing about alfalfa.

"I love it," he says. "It heals the land."

And so everywhere you look, except the upper hilltops and the wooded ridgelines, you're into a green carpet of alfalfa, a green sea of alfalfa, a green world of alfalfa, stretching to the hawk-guarded horizons.

Twenty, thirty feet and more below the carpet, the alfalfa roots burrow, spread and search for moisture, interlace and bind the soil, give stability to the soil, and let it heal.

Bud knows about land management and game management, maybe as much as Aldo Leopold knew, maybe more, some say, but he downplays his knowledge and is cool.

"What I know," he laughs, "is that you mustn't manage too much."

127

We sat in a boat on one of his homemade ponds and soaked up a little sun and a little beer and fished a little, for largemouth bass.

All around, the land stretched in the gauzy, delicate, newly budded, newly bloomy blush of Spring.

Bud said that after years of managing—"actually, after just planting the alfalfa and letting nature manage"—the land was thriving, as were its deer and grouse, rabbits, squirrels and songbirds. It was the best of all possible worlds: good hunting, good cash crop, and a good feeling about what you've done.

"This pond," Bud said, "this pond is the problem."

The pond looked good to me. Clumps of cattails; clear shallows shelving off into intriguing depths; weedfree waters glistening like a mini-lake, with little wavelets and everything. It looked even better after a chunky bass shot out and hit the plastic worm. It all seemed very natural.

"This pond was choked with weeds two years ago," Bud said. "Choked with milfoil. I had to kill it with chemicals. I didn't want to use them. I'm afraid of them."

I asked if the pond should be there at all.

True, if God had wanted a pond here, Bud replied, God would have put a pond here.

We fell silent and fished and sipped our beers.

"It's simple," Bud said finally. "That is what makes it so complex."

The Apostle: Gaylord Nelson

*T*he more I think about it, the more certain I am that this could be the best Christmas present I ever got.

And I'm not forgetting the Flexible Flyer sled still stored in the warehouse of my mind, still as cherished as anything labeled *Rosebud*.

I'm not forgetting my first fishing pole, either.

Or my first pool cue.

This present is not only as creative as one of Del Richardson's handtied girdle bugs, it's also as practical as a pair of his waders.

And completely unexpected, to boot.

"It's like discovering," says Steady Eddy, "that you have a whole smoked salmon left in the freezer when you thought you were fresh out."

Gaylord Nelson is going to head the Wilderness Society, the group that was organized in 1935 "for the one purpose of saving the wilderness remnants in America."

One of the cofounders was Wisconsin's immortal Aldo Leopold, and that's why this Christmas pleasures me so much. If ever two people talked each other's language, they are Gaylord Nelson and Aldo Leopold.

It doesn't suffice, Aldo set down in *Sand County Almanac*, just to have a society. Unless there be wilderness-minded men and women scattered through all the conservation bureaus, the society may never learn of new invasions until the time for action has passed.

"Furthermore," he emphasized, "a militant minority of wilderness-minded citizens must be on watch throughout the nation and available for action in a pinch."

Leading the drive to make the Apostle Islands a national park, Sen. Nelson was on watch way back in 1964 with a handful of friends that included Martin and Louie Hanson, Harold "Bud" Jordahl, and the irrepressible Sigurd Olson. Nelson warned:

> The deserted beaches of Lake Superior, the slumbering islands themselves and the thousands of acres in cool, green forest are in danger of being turned into another recreational slum such as we see in many parts of America. Land is cheap. Many owners are tempted to sell to any kind of buyer. If we fail to preserve a major section of our beautiful Northland almost immediately, we will sell out our citizens who love the beauty of nature and we will also sell out the future of Northern Wisconsin.

An Apostle Islands park, he argued, would make a logical link in a developing chain of natural resource facilities: Pictured Rocks and Sleeping Bear Dunes in Michigan, the bridge over the Straits of Mackinac, the Great Circle Highway around Lake Superior, the Voyageurs National Park proposal on the north shore of the lake, the Quetico-Superior Wilderness region, and Isle Royale National Park.

He was eloquent and he prevailed, but he prevailed because of something more than eloquence. Sigurd Olson once wrote in *Open Horizons*:

> To explain why anyone is a conservationist and what motivates him to the point where absorption in the preservation of the environment becomes a personal philosophy, means going back to the very beginning of his involvement with the natural scene.
>
> I believe one of the basic tenets for anyone really concerned is to have a love for the land, which comes through a long intimacy with natural beauty and living things, an association that breeds genuine affection and has an inherent understanding for its infinite and varied ecology.

John Lawton is not the only friend of Gaylord Nelson's to observe that inside the body of a U.S. Senator there always beats the heart of a little kid from Clear Lake, "goin' fishin' with a canepole."

"Only if there is understanding," Sig Olson observed, "can there be reverence, and only where there is deep emotional feeling is anyone willing to do battle."

Aldo Leopold put it pretty much the same way when he drew up his now-famous *Land Ethic*. He said that the ability to see the cultural value of wilderness boils down to a question of intellectual humility.

"The shallow-minded modern," Leopold said, "who has lost his rootage in the land, assumes that he has already discovered what is important; it is such who prate of empires, political or economic, that will last a thousand years."

That's where the humility came in, he pointed out. A land ethic changes the role of *Homo sapiens* from conqueror of the land-community to plain member and citizen. It implies respect for all the other members of the land-community. It implies respect and love for the environment.

"In the long pull," Gaylord Nelson said, "the most important issue that confronts mankind is *the environment.*"

Nelson has served us well: in the Wisconsin Assembly, as governor, as United States senator. He fought for the Apostle Islands and against the Vietnam War. He gave us Earth Day, and I have a hunch we ain't seen nothin' yet.

On Earth Day in 1970, Gaylord Nelson said in Madison that our goal was "an environment of decency, quality and mutual respect for all other human creatures, and for all other living creatures. . . ."

The Kid from Clear Lake is still in the ball game. That means we are, too.

Waiting for Death

*T*here must have been twenty crappies in the small school just below the surface of University Bay.

They hung, suspended and stilled, like some black-silver metallic mobile waiting for the merest whisper of wind to move and stir them into motion, into life.

I could have bent closer and touched them

I just bent closer and looked.

The body of each fish carried the brownish-whitish furry blotches of the fungus that would spread and cocoon them in death and disintegration. In this state, the fish no longer fed or even fled from man.

Marked for destruction, these fish still held their formation and waited for the end, serene as Buddha.

"The fungus," Cliff Brynildson would say later, "is *saprolegnia.* That's killing the crappies."

Brynildson is an area fish manager for the Department of Natural Resources and probably knows more about the Madison lakes than anybody this side of the baitshops.

What's going on with the crappie die-off is simple bookkeeping, Brynildson says. Ma Nature is balancing accounts.

"Remember," he reminds you, "we had a very large crappie hatch back in 1977 and '78. A *fantastic* hatch."

131

I remember. The Indian had complained to Steady Eddy that the hellgrammites they were using were bigger than the crappies they were catching.

"The fungus is a secondary infection," Brynildson explains, "the spawning stress leaves the fish in a weakened condition and they get infected."

I remember walking the Lake Michigan beaches when the dying alewives washed ashore in a singular solitude, their great bodies swathed in the white death, their great bodies now at the very perimeter of a reality as clear, as cold as the depths they had left forever.

"Lake Mendota seems to be hit the hardest," Brynildson said. "I would say eighty-five percent of our calls are concerned with Mendota."

"I would call DNR for you, too," I told the little immobile school of crappies. "I would call them and tell them about you and what's happening to you. but they already know about you and they are watching and waiting, only they really can't help you because this is out of their hands. You are in the hands of Somebody Else and that Somebody Else is not listed in our Directory."

"I would guess," Cliff Brynildson said quietly, "that fifteen to twenty per cent of all the crappies in the Madison lakes could be killed off by this fungus."

He emphasizes that this is only a guess.

He also emphasizes that no matter what the actual crappie die-off is, what's going on is *natural mortality*.

I don't know if the greater shock was hearing him say it, or seeing it written down.

"The most natural thing in this world," Steady says, "may be leaving it."

I watch the motionless crappies, waiting, and I am struck again at what a miraculous little machine a fish is, *any* fish. No one ever put it down better than Annie Dillard did in *Pilgrim at Tinker Creek*. She wrote:

> A whirling air in his swim bladder balances the fish's weight in the water; his scales overlap, his feathery gills pump and filter; his eyes work, his heart beats, his liver absorbs, his muscles contract in a wave of extending rip-

ples. The daphnias he eats have eyes and jointed legs. The algae the daphnias eat have green cells stacked like checkers or winding in narrow ribbons like spiral staircases up long columns of emptiness. And so on, diminishingly down. We have not yet found the dot so small it is uncreated, as it were, like a metal blank, or merely roughed in—and we never shall.

I pictured the crappies as metal blanks, pitted with rust.

Nature, Henry David Thoreau had observed, is mythical and mystical always, and spends her whole genius on the least work.

"The Creator," Dillard adds, "churns out the intricate texture of least works with a spendthrift genius and an extravagance of care."

We watch the dying crappies even as we watched the dying alewives and the dying brown trout and the eternal gulls. Only humans would speak of Nature's *least work*. Only humans would even attempt to define that work.

To wait as the fish wait, indeed as we all wait, is no small thing. The waiting may be the Great Work.

Secret of the Diseased Trees

Walking the woods in this season, Steady Eddy used to say, was like hanging out with naked people. "You see them with all their warts and wrinkles," he said. "Beauty is only bark deep."

Loren Eiseley observed in his hawk-eyed way that in this season all of Nature's pipes and tubing stood as exposed as the plumbing in your basement and now was a good time to see what Old Ma's secret was and maybe figure out how the machinery really worked.

I watched the snow dust the machinery until my eyes squinted to slits and I saw no secrets.

"Your eyes are OK," Steady reassures me. "It's the space between them that needs work."

What I saw was a lot of trees with holes in their trunks, galls on their bodies, silvery dead arms, fingers and branches.

Some of them appeared to be misshapen, appeared to be in pain. But maybe that's fanciful. I got the feeling that if these trees were people, they'd be hurting and you would hear them hurting. Old Folks with aches and pains.

These trees were what Aldo Leopold was writing about in *Sand County Almanac* when he said that after he bought his woods, he came to realize that he had also bought as many tree diseases as he had trees.

"My woodlot is riddled," was the way he put it, "by all the ailments that wood is heir to. I began to wish that Noah, when he loaded up the Ark, had left the tree diseases behind."

But it soon became clear to the Old Professor that those same diseases made his woodlot a mighty fortress, "unequaled in the whole country."

The list he drew up was a Mayo Clinic diagnosis for deadwood:

• His woods was headquarters for a family of raccoons; few of his neighbors had any. A fungus disease had weakened the roots of a maple, a storm had tipped it over and it offered a "bombproof" shelter for his seed stock of raccoons, without which hunters would have "cleaned them out."

• His woods housed a dozen ruffed grouse in downed windfalls of oaks. The cured oak retains its leaves, providing shelter and camouflage from wind, owl, fox and hunter. New twigs stung by a gall-wasp also provided grouse food.

• Each year the wild bees loaded up one of his hollow oaks with combs and that was made possible by the heart-rot of the tree. No heart-rot, no oaken hive.

• A flock of chickadees spent the whole year in his woods. In winter, every slab of dead bark was a treasury of eggs, larvae and cocoons. Every ant-tunneled heartwood bulged with milk and honey.

Wildlife depended on diseased trees, Aldo insisted. His pileated woodpecker chiseled living pines to extract fat grubs from diseased heartwood. His barred owl nested in a hollow basswood.

Loren Eiseley said the Secret could lie in the dead stalks and seedpods.

Aldo Leopold said that dead trees are "transmuted into living animals."

Steady Eddy says he used to think it was all for the birds, but maybe it's all for the bugs.

"You got a healthy tree, cut it down," Steady urges. "It's the sick ones that are doing all the work."

The Constancy of Worms

I stuck a pitchfork into the compost pile the other day—the first time since last Fall—and there they were. Worms. Hundreds of them. Waiting. Wriggling and working. And waiting. That's an even surer sign of Spring than the Blue Canoe emerging from the bottomless drifts.

I welcomed them back like long, silent friends.

In a world of inconstancy, worms are a great constancy. They do the world's thankless work and it takes a maturing before most men will admit the truth: *The living worm is more important to the work of Nature than the living man.*

Jerry Minnich, who is really into compost piles, tells me that there's *aerobic* composting and there's *anaerobic* composting—not to mention, strip composting, sheet composting, the Fourteen Day Method, the Indore Method, and God knows what all. I don't get too scientific or sophisticated.

I just stick table scraps and stuff in there that have a good chance of rotting—no plastics, glass or metal—make sure the raccoons and the neighbor's Malemute can't get into it and Ma Nature does the rest.

Leaf worms thrive in our pile. They're sort of bigger than red worms, smaller than nightcrawlers, and bluegills love them. Last summer when they were preparing for a weeklong fishing trip Up North, Vince and Ned dug up *a hundred-dozen* leaf worms from the pile and never worked up a sweat. Steady Eddy says he could put kids like that through college if only they signed with him and guaranteed exclusivity up to Waunakee and down to Stoughton.

Jerry, incidentally, not only wrote *A Wisconsin Garden Guide*, published by Stanton and Lee, but also *The Earthworm Book*, published by Rodale Press, a fascinating work that captures you right off by quoting the great English naturalist, Charles Darwin:

> The plough is one of the most ancient and most valuable of man's inventions; but long before he existed the land was in fact regularly ploughed and still continues to be thus ploughed by earthworms. It may be doubted whether there are many other animals which have played so important a part in the history of the world as have these lowly organized creatures.

You start thinking about that, and as Steady Eddy says, pretty soon you can't stop thinking about that.

I used to think worms were just for fishing.

Now I can't stop thinking about what worms are really for.

I even moved an old wooden lawn chair down beside the compost pile next to the great oaks. In the summertime, you can sit there in the shade and think about what's going on inside that trim, neat little pile.

Worms doing their work is what's going on. As they have always done their work. As they are supposed to do their work. They work with dead things. With corpses. With civilizations. With burial heaps. And they turn everything into compost if they can. That work may well be the most important in this world, for without it, this might be a world without table scraps at all. Not to mention you. Or me.

I find myself drawn to the compost pile more and more in this newly born Spring season. I turn over a forkful of rich, living soil and I watch. And I watch.

I go there now, even when I know I'm not going fishing at all.

Planting Fish

W e were sitting around Hugh Percy's Gasoline Emporium the other day just minding everybody's business and drinking that famous coffee that will rustproof you for life.

"We should go up and float the Brule this fall," Perce said, "when it gets cooler."

Perce always says escapist things like that when he's spent too much time with the brake system on the blue Chevette.

"I don't know what GM was thinking of when they tried that brake system," he says. "And they stuck with it for three years before they went back to their old brakes."

That in itself could make the blue Chevette as rare as the pucker-faced Edsel. And—please God—as valuable. You won't know for sure until Skip Frank phones during halftime some Sunday and asks casually if you're still driving that funny blue car with the training wheels.

Mechanics and plumbers, Steady Eddy often observes on the Catfish Flats, perform all the important work in our society; the rest of us are just winging it.

I tried to take Perce's mind off his problems by discussing somebody else's.

"Perce," I said, "did you hear about the DNR's troubles?"

"You mean with Rocky Raccoon and the Illinois people who owned it?"

"No," I said, "more troublesome than that."

"You mean with the couple from Iowa up north who got arrested for having four coolers full of panfish?"

"No," I said, "even more troublesome."

"Then I didn't hear."

"I heard on the radio," I said. "Carroll Besadny has a plan to cut back on the DNR staff. A couple of hundred employees."

God, I could almost hear Perce praying: not the nice truck-drivin' warden with the old-timey common sense who didn't arrest him that time on the Lemonweir River. That time when Perce showed him a bulging wallet full of licenses—Fishing, Hunting and Sportsman's—up to, but not including the year 1981. Nineteen eighty-one was in his other pants. At home.

137

"The radio report," I said, "didn't say who or when. It said only that the DNR secretary had a list of suggested personnel cuts because of the general belt-tightening that was going around and down."

"You know what they could cut?" Perce said. "What they *should* cut? They should cut out *planting* stuff."

"Trees," I said smartly.

"No, not trees," he said. "I'm thinking of stuff like trout and muskies and pheasants."

It costs an arm and a leg to raise these critters in captivity, Perce insisted, and when you stick them out in the wild you find you've got a breed of "sportsmen" out there following the hatchery truck around like imprinted geese following the farm collie.

"You raise artificial critters," Perce said, "catching them gets to be an artificial experience. It's unreal."

Aldo Leopold was saying the very same thing when he wrote in *A Sand County Almanac*:

> Consider, for example, a trout raised in a hatchery and newly liberated in an overfished stream. The stream is no longer capable of natural trout production. Pollution has fouled its waters, or deforestation and trampling have warmed or silted them. No one would claim that this trout has the same value as a wholly wild one caught out of some unmanaged stream in the high Rockies. Its esthetic connotations are inferior, even though its capture may require skill. Its liver, one authority says, is also so degenerated by hatchery feeding as to forebode an early death. Yet several overfished states now depend almost entirely on such man-made trout.

Aldo continues:

> Then, to safeguard this expensive, artificial and more or less helpless trout, the Conservation Commission feels impelled to kill all the herons and terns visiting the hatchery where it was raised, and all mergansers and otters inhabiting the stream in which it was released. The fisherman perhaps feels no loss in this sacrifice of one kind of wildlife for another, but the ornithologist is ready to bite off tenpenny nails.

Artificial management has, in effect, bought fishing at the expense of another and perhaps higher recreation: It has paid dividends to one citizen out of capital stock belonging to all.

I sat there on my wooden crate thinking of artificialized management.

Of pellet-raised trout that schooled like perch but sure as hell didn't taste like perch. Or trout, for that matter.

Of hatchery muskies that required forage fish seining operations in northern lakes to keep up with their feeding.

Of game farm pheasants, more delicate than barnyard chickens, and about as well-equipped to survive the Wisconsin Winter as your parakeet.

I remembered that Bud Jordahl, years ago when the winter storms literally blew down the Poynette pheasant operation, had suggested that the whole thing be permitted to die right then and there because it had simply outlived its usefulness.

"Put the money in habitat," Perce said. "Ma Nature will move in with the tenants."

Nothing wrong with going back to the drawing board every now and then, he claims. If GM has to do it, who doesn't?

Bulldozers and the Great Horned Owl

*T*he lawn party hadn't quite started and the host was sitting with the early birds under the sprawling tent top that bathed us all in golden light. We were discussing the difficulties of trying to maintain his little chunk of undeveloped country in a new wave of development that was washing over New Berlin, Wisconsin.

We had parked at the end of the road, below his driveway, and had wondered about the huge earth-moving machines, their treads clotted with soil and prairie grasses, a pride of them, silent in the weekend sun, sleeping now and passive as fed lions. We almost tiptoed around them.

"They're putting in houses," our host lamented. "Two-family units all along that hill."

"We tried to buy it," his wife would say later, "but we don't have that kind of money."

It was an old story, of course.

In the old days, only farmers lived out this far from Milwaukee—people who had to work the land for their living. Then, slowly, came the first of the people who didn't have to work the land for their living. They made their living in Milwaukee and in other places and they wanted to live out in the country because they loved the peace and quiet and the wildlife.

"We used to have a dozen pair of nesting pheasants," our host said. "Now, a single pair. They shot the rest."

Our host said that he had tried always to be a steward of the land since they moved out here. The pasture lands had gone back to wildflowers, the woods were coming back, and goldfinches and warblers flashed across the openings like bits of molten sunlight.

He didn't "tinker" too much with what nature was doing, he said. A birdhouse here, a clover-planted trail there. Clearing debris out of the creek every now and again to keep it open and flowing.

"I believe in what Aldo Leopold said," he declared in that quiet way Aldo's faithful have. "We are all members of an ecological community, and the private owner of land has an ethical obligation to maintain that community."

He said he argued before the local Planning Commission to put his land—and the land around it that was targeted for development—into conservancy.

"I took *Sand County Almanac* into a meeting," he recalled, "and I read what Aldo Leopold had said about 'a land ethic.' They didn't know what the hell *Sand County Almanac* was. They had never heard of it. They didn't know who the hell Aldo Leopold was. They thought I was crazy."

He knows that he is fighting a losing battle, that he is in the minority, literally a voice in the wilderness, arguing against the rush of development and tax base and concrete covering up his little creek. The bulldozers are at the bottom of his hill now, the bulldozers are at the bottom of everybody's hill in America now, and what America really needs is an Act of God.

He talks about the paradox of calling what is engulfing the wild places "civilization." It is "un-civilization," he insists. The conduct of its members is not "civil." It borders on the barbaric, the criminal.

"I can see shooting the pheasants," he said. "I think it's wrong, but if you need food and you're going to eat them, I can see it. But we had a Great Horned Owl that used to be part of the community, and somebody shot it and just left it. Now, what the hell is the sense of that? How can you make a case for that? Who the hell is going to eat a Great Horned Owl?"

"Scientists have an epigram," Aldo Leopold wrote in *Sand County Almanac*. "Ontology repeats phylogeny."

"What they mean," he explained, "is that the development of each individual repeats the evolutionary history of the race. This is true of mental as well as physical things. The trophy-hunter is the caveman reborn. Trophy hunting is the prerogative of youth, racial or individual, and nothing to apologize for."

Perhaps the Great Horned Owl was killed by youths who had never killed anything before, or perhaps it was killed by adults who no longer keep track of the things they have killed. In any event, our host pointed out, the owl was simply blasted out of his sitting-tree, and we are all diminished by the senseless act.

The disquieting thing in the modern picture, Aldo Leopold said, was the trophy-hunter who never grows up, in whom the capacity for isolation, perception and husbandry is undeveloped or perhaps lost. Aldo wrote:

> He is the motorized ant who swarms the continents before learning to see his own backyard, who consumes, but never creates, outdoor satisfactions. For him the recreational engineer dilutes the wilderness and artificializes its trophies in the fond belief that he is rendering a public service.
>
> The trophy recreationist has peculiarities that contribute in subtle ways to his own undoing. To enjoy, he must possess, invade, appropriate. Hence the wilderness he cannot see has no value to him. Hence the universal

assumption that an unused hinterland is rendering no service to society. To those devoid of imagination, a blank place on the map is a useless waste; to others, the most valuable part.

Recreational development is a job not of building roads into lovely country, but of building receptivity into the still unlovely mind.

On the way out, we passed the sleeping bulldozers, which first thing Monday morning would crush baby rabbits in the nests where they had always been safe and secure, even from the Great Horned Owl.

TRIBAL ELDERS

Frank Lloyd Wright

We were driving back from the boonies the other day and, as we do whenever we're near Spring Green, we swung across the Wisconsin River and paid our respects to Frank Lloyd Wright.

Frank Lloyd Wright taught me one of the most valuable lessons I ever learned in this life, and it had nothing to do with architecture. ("You can barely live in a house," Steady Eddy points out, "let alone design one.")

Frank Lloyd Wright is still such a force on earth that it's hard to believe he left it almost twenty-five years ago. "Twenty-five years after his death," the *New York Times* reported two weeks ago, "this will be the season of Frank Lloyd Wright."

The *Times* explained that an exhibition of photographs, decorative objects and furniture from Mr. Wright's early years had opened at the Cooper-Hewitt Museum—"getting an end-of-summer jump on the fall season"—and on September 16, an array of original Wright drawings went on exhibition at the Max Protech Gallery. Unlike any other Frank Lloyd Wright exhibition in memory, this one offers its objects for sale.

The Protech Gallery is serving as a vehicle for the Frank Lloyd Wright Foundation, inheritor of Wright's architectural practice and conservator of his archives, which has decided to start selling off some of "the Master's possessions" as a way of building an endowment to help preserve Taliesin, Wright's house and studio in Spring Green.

Behind you, Taliesin overlooks the quiet valley, not unlike a Tibetan lamasery, ageless, timeless. In the very same instant the patina disappears like morning mist and Taliesin stands newborn, as though it had just been completed yesterday.

In front of you, the legend on Frank Lloyd Wright's grave reads: "Love of an idea is love of God."

It happened during one of those recurring campaigns to convince the citizens of Madison to support the construction of the Frank Lloyd Wright-designed Monona Terrace project, a great Civic Center that would be built on the Law Park site and extend over Lake Monona's prime shore. "You know," Steady Eddy says, "right across the railroad tracks where they park all the cars now."

Mr. Wright himself was going around trying to persuade Madison voters that they should authorize, by referendum, the funding of such a unique, not to say magnificent, civic project.

Eventually, the state legislature, supporting a cabal of local conservative politicians, decreed that there could be no construction on the site higher than twenty feet, but that is another story. It also explains, as Studs Terkel puts it, why "Republicans don't write folksongs."

This night found Mr. Wright on a local TV station, live, to answer questions put by the young host—this was pre-blow-dried, you understand—impeccably groomed, sitting atop his high stool as casually as Dave Garroway, holding his clipboard confidently as he smiled his welcome to us. Mr. Wright, with white hair, flowing ascot and the general mien of a schoolmaster, was poised, pointer in hand, in front of more charts than the Seven-Foot Nun had employed in explaining the Crusades in the Dark Ages before Hollywood finally got around to doing it.

The host assured us that the whole community had questions for Mr. Wright, and ours would be welcome indeed during the broadcast. If we called the superimposed telephone number, people in the control room would take down our questions and bring them into the studio later in the program. The host thanked us again, introduced Mr. Wright, thanked *him* again, and then looked down at his clipboard and read off the first question.

Instantly, Mr. Wright, who had been absolutely immobile during the preliminaries, flew into action. He was a dynamo, talking and pointing, flipping charts, explaining renderings and drawings and sketches. I don't know if it was enlightening. It was impressive. Here's this old guy, this Living Legend, careening around like a whirling dervish, yet cool as Fred Astaire. The camera moved in, trying to figure him out, trying to follow him, to track with him, trying its level best to cope with genius in a little television studio.

It went on for a very long time: I could visualize caissons in the very bed of Lake Monona underpinning the structure; actors from exotic places who would play in the Terrace theaters; the veritable Taj Mahal itself built as a temple of love to a city by its citizens. When Mr. Wright finished, he stood immobile again, the pointer held at Port Arms like a rifle.

The host beamed. He smiled at us and at Mr. Wright and said how interesting that answer was. Then he looked at his clipboard again and asked his second question. Mr. Wright never moved a muscle, never moved his pointer.

"I thought I just answered that," Mr. Wright said. *"Weren't you listening?"*

I thought: *My God. How cruel. How heartless. How insensitive. The host wasn't Dave Garroway anymore.*

Sure, Studs Terkel might have been gentler, but Frank Lloyd Wright was right. The kid had asked *one question* and Wright had answered *his next six*. And if you intend to make a living asking people questions, you had damn well better *listen* to their answers.

I interviewed Mr. Wright six months before he died. I hung on every word, every breath. I listened so hard my ears hurt.

Loren Eiseley

We had a death in the family last week.
And now there is a void in our hearts as vast as the ones left by the passing of Baba Jula. And then by the passing of her loving Old Country husband, Grandpa Vincent. And then by the passing of their great bear of a son-in-law, Frano, The Old Man himself.

Loren Eiseley is dead.

The notice in last Monday's edition of the *Milwaukee Journal* was sparse, brief under the heading: Deaths in Other Places:

"Loren C. Eiseley, anthropologist, Saturday in Philadelphia. Expert on Darwinian theory and human evolution."

And that was it.

The Old Bone Picker, as he described himself, would have loved the economy of it. The author of a half-dozen of the best books ever written on the evolution of life reported now by death and the always dry-eyed wire services in a sliver of a sentence, in thirteen words, a few wisps of smoke rising from the last of the dying embers.

It is strange how you can feel a sadness for a Being you never met, never listened to, never talked to.

Yet of course, anyone who ever read Loren Eiseley did meet him, did listen to him, and did talk to him.

His books bear the titles that whisper of far-away worlds and endless, endless corridors of time: *The Immense Journey, The Invisible Pyramid, The Unexpected Universe.* The words must contain some encrypted genetic code that communicates with our very souls.

It is not necessary to ride over a mountain range, Loren Eiseley wrote in *The Firmament of Time*, to experience historical infinity. It can descend upon one in the lecture room.

I find it is really in daylight that the sensation I am about to describe is apt to come most clearly upon me, and for some reason, I associate it extensively with crowds. It is not, you understand, an hallucination. Here is the way it comes:

I mount the lecturer's rostrum to address a class. Like any workworn professor fond of his subject, I fumble among my skulls and papers, shuffle to the blackboard and back again, begin the patient translation of three billion years of time into chalk scrawls and uncertain words ventured timidly to a sea of young, impatient faces. Time does not frighten them, I think enviously. They have, most of them, never lain awake and grasped the sides of a cot, staring upward into the darkness while the slow clock strokes begin.

"Doctor," a voice diverts me. I stare out near-sightedly over the class. A hand from the back row gesticulates. "Doctor, do you believe there is direction to evolution?" Instead of the words, I hear a faint piping, and see an eager scholar's face squeezed dissolving on the body of a chest-thumping ape. "Doctor, is there a direction?"

I see it then—the trunk that stretches monstrously behind him. It winds out of the door, down dark and obscure corridors to the cellar and vanishes into the floor. It writhes, it crawls, it barks and snuffles and roars, and the odor of the swamp exhales from it. That pale young scholar's face is the last bloom on a curious animal extrusion through time. And who among us, under the cold persuasion of the archaeological eye, can perceive which of his many shapes is real, or if, perhaps, the entire shape in time is not a greater and more curious animal than its single appearance?

I too am aware of the trunk that stretches loathsomely back of me along the floor. I too am a many-visaged thing that climbed upward out of the dark of endless leaf falls and has slunk, furred, through the glitter of blue glacial nights. I, the professor, trembling absurdly on the platform with my book and spectacles, am the single philosophical animal. I am the unfolding worm, and mud fish, the weird tree of Igdrasil shaping itself endlessly out of the darkness toward the light.

I have said this is not an illusion. It is when one sees in this manner, or in a sense of strangeness one halts on a busy street to verify the appearance of one's fellows that one knows a terrible new sense has opened a faint crack on the Absolute. It is in this way alone that one comes to grips with a great mystery, that life and time bear some curious relationship to each other that is not shared by inanimate things.

It is in the brain that this world opens. To our descendants it may become a commonplace, but me, and others like me, it has made a castaway. I have no refuge in time, as others do who troop homeward at nightfall. As a result, I am one of those who linger furtively over coffee in the kitchen at bedtime or haunt the all night restaurants.

. . .

Loren Eiseley's body has gone back into the ground he knew better than most. The rest of him still lives, still teaches—better than most.

Colin Fletcher

"*I* find that the truly great times for thinking thoughts," Colin Fletcher once said, "are when I am standing in the shower, sitting on the john, or walking. And the greatest of these, by far, is walking."

Steady Eddy would throw in bass fishing, but he's not militant about it. Walking, Steady figures, is something pitchers do when they can't control their best stuff, and, incidentally, if you're putting batters on base that way you might as well plunk them so they aren't feeling they got something for nothing.

Colin Fletcher is one of the world's great walkers. Born in Wales and educated in England, he moved to this country in the fifties and became a legend.

He wrote *The Thousand Mile Summer*, an account of his walk from California to Canada. He wrote *The Man Who Walked Through Time*, an account of his trip on foot through the length of the Grand Canyon; and he wrote the definitive books on hiking: *The Complete Walker*, and the revised, enlarged, updated *The New Complete Walker* (Knopf).

It's the hiker's Bible, as any old professional will tell you. If you're just breaking in your first boots, I commend Colin Fletcher to you.

In response to the question "Why walk?" he answers that walking hones not only body, but your mind as well. It gets you to remembering that happiness had something to do with simplicity.

"And so, by slow degrees," he says, "you regain a sense of harmony with everything you move through—rock and soil, plant and tree and cactus, spider and fly and rattlesnake and coyote, drop of rain and racing cloud shadow."

You have long outgrown the crass assumption, he says, with his waffle stompers firmly on the ground, that the world was made for man.

After a while, he predicts, you find that you are gathering the whole untidy but glorious mishmash of sights and sounds and smells and touches and tastes and emotions that tumble through your recent memory.

"Then you begin to connect those ciphers," he says, "one with the other. And once you begin to connect, only to connect, nothing can stop you. . . ."

I was connecting ciphers in the Arboretum as usual the other day. Past the Redwing Marsh and not a fisherman on Wingra. Through the Gallistel Woods and not a mosquito on my bare arms. The straight-line walk through the Longenecker Horticultural Gardens—from the Hoopes blue spruce to the Manchurian winterberry—and on to the Curtis prairie. Up ahead on the path, a group of students clustered around its instructor. I stopped, just leaned on the walking staff.

From where I stood I couldn't hear the instructor.

From where they stood, the students couldn't see me.

They couldn't see the weasel, slipping out of the prairie across the path not fifteen feet behind their backs. Self-possessed. Cool as a pickpocket leaving a crowd.

We didn't make eye contact, yet there was that flash Annie Dillard had captured in her book, *Teaching a Stone to Talk*:

> Weasel: I had never seen one wild before. He was ten inches long, thin as a curve, a muscled ribbon, brown as fruitwood, soft-furred, alert. His face was fierce, small and pointed as a lizard's; he would have made a good arrowhead. . . . He had two black eyes I didn't see, any more than you can see a window. The weasel was stunned

151

into stillness as he was emerging from beneath an enormous shaggy wildrose bush four feet away. I was stunned into stillness, twisted backward on the tree trunk. Our eyes locked, and someone threw away the key.

Please do not tell me about 'approach-avoidance conflicts.' I tell you I've been in that weasel's brain for sixty seconds and he was in mine.

When I excused myself past the students and headed for the Leopold Pines, the instructor's voice floated after me: "... that's last year's growth. Notice the leaves and the photosynthetic ..."

Gordon MacQuarrie

*I*n a boyhood pantheon of heroes, Gordon MacQuarrie was one of my favorites.

This in no way slights Ted Gullic, the "Old Reliable" of the then-American Association Milwaukee Brewers, who terrorized Triple A pitching but who could never stick in the majors.

Or Don Hutson, the hipless Green Bay Packer who moved through the hapless Chicago Bear secondary like an otter through a trout hatchery.

Or Father Alphonse Kohler, the assistant priest over at Holy Assumption who charmed the Ladies' Sodality right out of its sensible shoes and whose proficiency with a shotgun was an inspiration to all of us who aspired to be good priests and good wing shots, not necessarily in that order.

The beauty of Gordon MacQuarrie was that he was a writer, and what he wrote about was the outdoors.

He was the outdoor editor of the *Milwaukee Journal* for twenty years, and he got paid to go hunting and fishing and bumming around in the Wisconsin boonies, and when he wrote about it in the *Journal* something magical happened. Gordon MacQuarrie was the North Country as was his wondrous fictitious organization, the Old Duck Hunters Association, Inc. (the Inc. stood for incorrigible), consisting of MacQuarrie, the chronicler; and his real-life father-in-law, the chroniclee.

On the printed page, his father-in-law, Al Peck, a car dealer from Superior, became the immortal duck-skiffing, trout-stalking old reprobate, the brown mackinaw-clad "Mister President" with whom MacQuarrie and his readers shared the American Dream, the same dream Huck Finn shared with Tom Sawyer, that Butch shared with Sundance, that Steady Eddy shares with the world.

"Many times I have watched Mister President," Gordon MacQuarrie wrote, "in duck blinds, on trout streams, in upland bird cover, in deer woods—and have come to believe that the things of the outdoors which he symbolizes are a way of life."

"Mister President" first came to national prominence in the pages of *Sports Afield*, and he lives on in the anthology, *Stories of the Old Duck Hunters and Other Drivel*, compiled and edited by Zack Taylor, MacQuarrie's "friend and fan."

It is in this anthology, published by Stackpole Books of Harrisburg, Pennsylvania, that MacQuarrie's genius for what is now called "environmental communication" is on display for all to marvel at.

It's like sneaking a peek into Mister President's creel as he hauls himself out of the Brule River, bitten and bludgeoned by adversity, tested beyond mortal endurance, yet as triumphant as Don Hutson ever was.

Trout waters can be very personal places. The best trout streams are the ones you grow up with and then grow old with. Eventually they become like a familiar shotgun, or a faithful old setter or comfortable pair of shoes. You develop a profound affection for them, and you think maybe before you die you will even understand a little about them.

We went downstream, he on the right bank, I on the left. At this putting-in place, high above the right bank, stretches the level top of an old logging railroad grade. The light was waning in the west, and the top of this embankment cut off the sky like a knife. Below this ran the churning river, far noisier and more mysterious than it had been an hour before.

Certainly you must know how it is to come to a place like this. A place you know well. A place where you are

153

on intimate terms with the smallest boulders, where yonder projecting limb once robbed you of a choice fly, where from beneath the undercut banks, the big ones prowl by night to claim the larger morsels of the darkness.

Strange and utterly irresistible are such places to trout fishermen. There you had hold of a good one. Here you netted a smaller one. Down beyond the turn in the pool below the old snag pile, you lost still another. The spell of the approaching night silenced the President, but not for long.

"One thing I can't figure out," he said finally. His voice came to me from a point downstream, drifting over the purring waters in the sweet June air. "How can a Scotch Presbyterian like you enjoy anything that's so much fun?"

He vanished into the gloom like some wise and ancient spirit of the river. I heard his wader brogues nick a rock as he stumbled, heard him cuss softly and then the river took me in. . . .

But it is something to be alone in the bush with a .30-.30 under your arm, the wind in the trees and the feeling that if there are such things as big cities, they must have existed in some ancient past. It is a fine thing to climb a rise, sit in the tumbleweeds, smoke a pipe and look off for miles at more of the same country you just came through.

Some people ask why men go hunting. They must be the kind of people who seldom get far from the highways. What do they know of the tryst a hunting man keeps with the wind and the trees and the sky? Hunting? The means are greater than the end and every hunter knows it.

Gordon MacQuarrie died, at fifty-six, in 1956.

He is quoted extensively here because the Wisconsin Academy of Sciences, Arts and Letters—in its inexplicable wisdom—has seen fit to present North Country Notebook with an award in the name of Gordon MacQuarrie.

And I wanted you to share our feeling for what that name means.

Sigurd Olson

When I was with the *Capital Times* back in 1977, Miles McMillin decided the paper could justify a trip up to Ely, Minnesota, to interview Sigurd Olson. Then in his late seventies, Sigurd was again involved in a fight to preserve the Boundary Waters Canoe Area.

We did a three-part series with Sigurd, and I regard the experience as one of the most illuminating of my life. He was the spiritual father of us all, including our daughter Marty, who accompanied me on that memorable trip and who also recalled it when the radio announced the other morning that Sigurd F. Olson had died at age eighty-two in his beloved North Country while trying out a new pair of snowshoes.

Hugh Percy, Steady Eddy, and everyone who loved Sigurd Olson agree with the words spoken by Sig's friend Les Blacklock, the wilderness photographer and writer who collaborated with Sigurd on the book, *The Hidden Forest*.

"Any sorrowing we do is not for Sig," Les said. "It is for us."

Of Sigurd's death on snowshoes, Les observed: "He wouldn't have wanted to slow down and spend a lot of time in bed."

When we were up with Sigurd, he had spoken of death in that measured, matter-of-fact way he had. He told of the old Indian legend that said you knew you were going to die when you heard the owl call your name.

He said he hadn't heard it yet, but he was still listening.

Marty says she remembers it the same way.

Sigurd had a profound influence on her. She probably would have discovered the Boundary Waters eventually, as so many young people do, but being in his house and hearing his voice may have hastened the process.

"The many young people who come through here," Sigurd said, "they're going into the wilderness now trying to find something bigger than themselves—something sacred. Something the Indians sensed long before we came here.

"They had the sacred places where they didn't speak, just as we have it in our great cathedrals and in our places of worship.

"They had it on the Kawashaway, the land they called 'No Place Between.' They had it on Darkey Lake. They had it on LaCroix. They tried to epitomize in such places that there were values which they felt deeply about. They tried to put those values into words long before there was such a thing as a written language. And the legends have come down."

He discussed the early caves of France and Spain in which the early people had painted pictures, *sacred* pictures, legends. The early people were all animists at heart, he said. The spirit world was in everything.

"So when people go into the wilderness today," he continued, "where there's any left unravished by noise, by mechanical motors, they are looking for the same spiritual inspiration the early people found. And many of them today, more than ever before, are finding it again.

"They find it in the sense of harmony and oneness with all living things. They find it in a feeling of communion and meditation. And, as I said in one of my books, one doesn't have to be a Buddhist to meditate, or get into any special position. Just looking at any natural thing is, in a sense, meditation. It is communion with God, or the Spirit. I think that's what people are looking for in the wilderness today, spiritual values. And they are almost impossible to define."

Sigurd said it was this feeling, this sense of harmony, that the Boundary Waters Canoe Area represented, along with other wilderness areas. He also admitted that the problem with saving wilderness was that not all people absorbed the wilderness values.

"Some people go into the bush," he allowed, "and come out and never get the spiritual at all. *Intangible* values," he said, "are difficult to explain."

Once in Germany, he recalled, during World War II, along a stretch of the River Main—"ruined buildings all around—the stench of death everywhere"—he saw a flock of mallard ducks come flying down the river as they had always done.

"That flock of mallards," Sig smiled, "was an intangible value. And all of a sudden I was back in the North Country."

156

He insisted that the whole business of conservation and preservation was based on those intangible values.

"You must understand," Sigurd Olson said that springtime morning in northern Minnesota, "that in saving the Boundary Waters Canoe Area—in saving any wilderness area—you are saving more than rocks and trees and mountains and lakes and rivers.

"What you are really saving is the human spirit.

"What you are really saving is the human soul."

I look at the photograph of Sigurd Olson and he gazes at me like some guru—wise, benign, his very Being full of the knowledge that waits for us beyond the cities where the bush begins. I close my eyes and he is still there, dressed now for the Northern Winter, standing on the new snowshoes in the quiet drifted valley. And in the dazzling stillness the brilliant bundle of feathers is calling his name.

Calvin Rutstrum

*I*t was a another short, dry-eyed item tucked into the interior of the *Milwaukee Journal* the other day. "Canoe export dies at 86."

The dateline was Marine on St. Croix, Minn. The source was the Associated Press.

"Calvin Rutstrum, who prepared countless future disci ples for canoe travel in his book, *The Way of the Wilderness*, has died at the age of 86, it was announced Thursday.

"He died Feb. 5 at Ladd Memorial Hospital in Osceola, Wis., after a long illness. Announcement of his death was delayed at the request of his wife, Florence."

The obituary went on to state that his fifteen books "describe his profound enchantment with the wilderness and instruct readers on preparing for conducting remote canoe trips.

"Rutstrum stayed close to the wilderness, writing mostly at his cabin on Cloud Bay, Ontario, near Pigeon River. He made frequent, extensive journeys into the Canadian wilderness by canoe, and in the winter traveled on dogsleds and snowshoes."

157

There are many people who will not mourn the passing of Calvin Rutstrum because they never knew him.

We come and go like the ripples on a stream and there are too many to keep track of, too many to mourn.

The canoe nut, the voyageur, the crows-footed aficionado usually discovers Calvin Rutstrum the way one discovers a feeder stream and is forever after enchanted.

Perhaps, if it hadn't been for Sigurd Olson out in the main channel, Calvin wouldn't have been relegated to the feeder crick, but that's the way it is in Ma Nature's game. It's tougher than hell for the little trees to grow when they're planted in the shadow of the big tree. And Sigurd Olson was a mighty big tree.

Sigurd was a more poetic writer than Calvin and certainly captured the essence of canoeing the Quetico-Superior, the fabled Boundary Waters Canoe Area, as not even a camera lens can capture it.

But Calvin, like a lot of old North Country coots who were Up There before snowmobiles and floatplanes, is as practical as cast-iron fry pans and flannel longjohns.

I remember a van ride up to Nakina, Ontario, where the bush pilot waited, and all the way up, Karl Schmidt—when it wasn't his shift to drive—was reading to us from Calvin's *North American Canoe Country*, the complete guide to canoeing: techniques, routes, outfitting and equipment.

> Until now, the pressures and excitement of fast-water canoe travel have dominated your course—a succession of adventures which have not been the wilderness solitude you had envisioned. But finally, beyond the rapids, you discover that the river has lost most of its fury, flowing around curve after curve, past little green islands that look like green-masted ships slowly heading for the sea. You hear only the rhythmic dip of your paddle in this imposing hush. An occasional bad stroke bangs the paddle against the canoe, and you are shocked—and embarrassed at breaking the silence. *This* is the solitude you dreamed about.

And that's about as poetic as Calvin gets.

Most times he gives you all the nuts-and-bolts stuff, stuff that you can stick in your duffel and use when you're back in the boonies:

> A tumpline simply consists of two eight-foot latigo leather straps sewn to a wider leather head strap. The head strap should fit on top and forward of the head, just above the forehead—not *on* the forehead. . . .

> Most canoe voyageurs eventually get around to wearing lightweight wool underwear. The clammy feel of cotton on wet, cold days usually decides the issue. The two-piece style is my choice; the shirt, a crew-neck pullover type. Much of the time, the only upper garment I wear is the undershirt. I try to get it in red so it looks like an outer garment—and it shows up well in color photography. . . .

> Never carry tent, sleeping bags or air mattresses in packsacks or duffel bags. It is exasperating to stuff these bulky items into, and pull them out of, tight packs at every camp.

The beauty of Rutstrum is that you can disagree with him every now and again, but you never reject him, because he is your connection to a bygone age, an eyewitness to that storied North that voyageurs still seek.

"There is pure art," he writes, "in watching a lone Indian travel and camp with a tea pail, knife, fishline, rifle, rabbitskin blanket, canoe and paddle. The Indian sleeps in the blanket under the canoe, lives off the country, performing each act with incredible simplicity."

I remember now Sandy Nate, the Cree out of Fort Hope who guided us down the Wabassi to its confluence with the mighty Albany and then to Ogoki Post. Around the campfire he spoke of what the wilderness meant to him, and it was a comfort to realize that the old coot Rutstrum had that right, too:

> Only those who awake at dawn alone in a wilderness can know the thoughts and feelings of the solitary traveler. At the first sign of wakefulness, you are seized with a sudden realization that for many hours you have lain unconscious and isolated in the wilderness. It is a strange and rare experience. . . .

Now Calvin has joined Sigurd and Sandy beyond the Open Horizons. Thank God they left their maps and charts and books and stuff.

John Muir

We were up in John Muir country with Marion Moran the other day watching the great goose flights bugling over the crisp hills like loosened hound dogs on the hunt.

As we skirted Ennis Lake—the "Fountain Lake" of John Muir's boyhood—the very air rang with the vibrations of the past.

The air rings the same way on the Wisconsin River at Sauk City, where you expect to see Augie Derleth walking the railroad trestle.

The air rings at Aldo Leopold's Shack in the "sand county."

It rings all through Sigurd Olson's North Country.

Some call it "The Pipes of Pan," the voice of Earth. Some say it is the spirit essence of the person who once walked this place, clinging like burrs and sticktights to the clothing of newcomers.

John Muir once walked in this place. And it sings.

Before he went off to the University in Madison where a memorial stone acknowledges his passage; before a glacier in Alaska and a redwood grove in California were named after him; before he became "the father of our National Park System," he walked *this* place.

John Muir was a boy here, and growing up under his Scots father couldn't have been all sunfish and wild berry-picking.

"His father was harsh," Marion said. "That was the way then. Sometimes you think it's a miracle that John Muir grew up to become what he did."

Linnie Marsh Wolfe, in her biography, *The Life of John Muir* (University of Wisconsin Press) tells of the time the Muir family was digging a well and his father sent young John down in a bucket to chisel through the hard sandstone.

So the boy hacked away, day after day, by the light of a candle lantern, at the bottom of the three-foot bore.

One morning, when the well was nearly eighty feet deep, a deathlike faintness seized him. He called feebly for help. His father, leaning over the top, heard him and sharply commanded him to get back in the bucket. John, slumping into it, was hauled up and carried into the house, unconscious.

Already it was being said among the neighbors: "Old Man Muir works his children like cattle."

The next day, the boy was in the well again. When he had chiseled out ten additional feet, he struck the nether springs with an abundance of pure water.

As a grown man, John Muir recounted that brush with death in his autobiography, *The Story of My Boyhood and Youth*:

Once, I was let down into a deep well into which choke-damp carbonic acid gas had settled and nearly lost my life. The deeper I was immersed in the invisible poison, the less capable I became of willing measures of escape from it. And in just this condition are those who toil or dawdle or dissipate in crowded towns, in the sinks of commerce or pleasure.

The iron entered John Muir's soul, Wolfe judges, when he saw "pious people" ruthless in their treatment of human beings and animals in their charge. It caused him to revolt, early, against religion.

"His first active rebellion," she writes, "stemmed from his father's callousness in overdriving the horse, Nob, to get from one religious meeting to another.

"When the poor beast, slowly dying of pneumonia, followed them about the farm as if dumbly pleading for help, John began seriously to question a religion so devoid of love.

"Another grief came when his father sold their pony, Jack, to someone bound for the California goldmines. The money that he got for the pony meant more to the father than the happiness of his children."

The trail widened and the flattened gentians in the deep tire tracks made you hurt. A four-wheel-drive vehicle had twisted and powered through here as cruelly as a thing devoid of love.

161

The air rang with violence.

I straightened up a few of the gentians and leaned them against their clumpmates.

They stood like walking wounded, in shock.

That was the horror of the ATVs, Marion said, the All Terrain Vehicles. They got into the back country and just tore up plant communities that took years and years to stabilize. The ATVs upset a natural balance in the backwoods and set off a disruptive, destructive cycle that continued long after they were on the paved roads, their bumpers trailing grass of Parnassus, the fringed gentians mashed down in their mud cleats.

Marion pointed to the erosion starting to gully the hillside, tiny feeder cricks coming into the main channel. The land was coming apart here, fissured, veined.

Do the drivers of ATVs know who John Muir was?

Would it make any difference?

John Muir's admonition to the ATV mentalities of his time is reported by Linnie Marsh Wolf in her book, *John of the Mountains*:

> Nearly all our forests in the West are on mountains and cover and protect the fountains of the rivers. They are being more and more invaded and, of course, fires are multiplied; five to ten times as much lumber is burned as is used, to say nothing of the waste of lowlands by destructive floods. As sheep advance, flowers, vegetation, grass, soil, plenty, and poetry vanish.

One way to see John Muir country is in the company of naturalist Marion Moran. It may be the best way.

August Derleth

Some friends of Augie Derleth got together the other day in Sauk City to mark the tenth anniversary of his death, and everybody who was there loved it.

Including Augie.

He was there, all right: bigger than life, bigger than death, his presence in the village, in the countryside, as real as the living river that moves like time itself through this timeless country.

They're calling it "Derleth Country" now. Not just the scholars from the universities, but the shopkeepers, too. Augie is the local boy who made good by never leaving the locality. His writing is being "discovered" and "rediscovered." His book *Walden West* is being hailed as "an American classic" vindicating *The New York Times*, which said as much when the book first appeared.

Time is not only vindicating but making a prophet of Sinclair Lewis, who predicted almost fifty years ago that one day people would come visiting August Derleth's Sauk City in the same way people go visiting Charles Dickens' London and Nathaniel Hawthorne's Salem.

"I felt," Lewis said of Augie's *Prairie Saga*, "something pretty important in the wind, something that will go far beyond Wisconsin, and I thought how important it would be for Wisconsin to discover its own young man before the rest of the world discovers him and asks Wisconsin why they had not!"

Professor Emeritus Bob Gard was saying pretty much the same thing when he observed in that laconic way of his that it was just too bad the University of Wisconsin had never seen fit to acknowledge Augie with an honorary doctorate, and maybe the school would get around to it now.

"The University treated Frank Lloyd Wright the same way," Prof. Gard said, "so that's pretty good company."

Edna Meudt, who has written so many beautiful things for Augie, chose instead to read Jesse Stuart's "Letter to August Derleth."

> Dear Augie,
> Since you have gone on a long journey,
> I don't have your new address.
> It's not like you not to send it to me.
> But this is like old times when I used to write to you,
> To your favorite place on earth, Sauk City, Wisconsin.
> Augie, where are you now? What is your new address?
> And what are you doing? You must be doing something.
> I know you could never sit still . . .

Edna paused, because no one who knew August Derleth can hear Jesse Stuart's letter read aloud and not have something happen inside. Because Jesse's words captured Augie, they captured us.

> You were Wisconsin, two yards wide,
> A block of a man, two-hundred-fifty pounder,
> Barrel-chested, protruding chin and jutted jaw . . .
> And books, you were one hundred-fifty plus
> And Nature's walking Encyclopedia.
> Hell, how can a grave hold you?
> You were a voice, Wisconsin's voice,
> You were a personality; you were everything
> Of man, all together at once,
> Unforgettable, genius extraordinary.
> You never created a character to equal you.

Pete Blankenheim, Augie's lifelong friend, described him as "a big burly-chested man sitting by the brook trestle with his head cocked to the side, listening for the sound of birds."

"He was a complex man," his friend from boyhood George Marx says. "Lots of sides to him."

"He knew all about the plants and birds," Hugo Schwenker says. "And he knew all about the people, too."

At the cemetery, before the graveside service, George Marx cheerfully took me on a tour.

"These are all Aug's friends and neighbors buried here," he said. "All the people he wrote about. We're buried over here."

He led the way to the Marx family area, and sure enough there was George's headstone, the date of death left blank.

The sense of community is strong here. These people were together in classrooms, church services, free thinker meetings. And here they are, together again. The author and the characters. And then the realization comes like a bolt: *They were all the authors: Augie just happened to write it down.*

At the end of the services, everybody bowed in a silent prayer and I watched the blue sky for hawks. When one appeared, I nudged Hugo Schwenker. He didn't seem surprised, not even when a second hawk appeared. And then a third. High up. Circling, circling.

Chief Seattle

*I*t was, in my humble opinion, some kind of high-water mark in outdoor journalism.

In its first Sunday paper of the new year, the *Milwaukee Journal* devoted over thirty-four column inches of text to the words of Chief Seattle responding to President Franklin Pierce in the year 1853.

The occasion was the arrival at Puget Sound of Isaac Stevens, newly appointed governor of the Washington Territory, with an offer from the President. The offer to the Indians of the area was to purchase from them two million acres of land for $150,000, and the Indians were then to vacate the land.

The formal offer to buy was made in front of a crowd gathered at the general store.

"Chief Seattle knew full well what the Indians' choices were," the *Journal* stated in its preface. "His reply gives us much to think about, even 130 years later." This is what Chief Seattle told the President's man:

> We may be brothers after all. We shall see. One thing we know, which the white man may one day discover— our God is the same God. You may think now that you own Him as you wish to own our land, but you cannot. He is the God of man and his compassion is equal for the red man and the white. The Earth is precious to Him and to harm the Earth is to heap contempt on its Creator. The white man too shall pass, perhaps sooner than all other tribes. Continue to contaminate your bed, and you will one night suffocate in your own waste. . . .

The piece was titled "The Sacred Land." The subtitle was: "For Chief Seattle and his people this land was their lifeblood." A three-column illustration showed a contemplative Indian chief surrounded by animals, waters, forest, mountains, and a soaring eagle.

I intuited that outdoor editor Ron Leys was going to draw a lot of heat for this one, so I called him and congratulated him on printing it.

He said he was drawing a lot of heat for this one.

He said he'd had Chief Seattle's words around for years, hoping to drop them into the paper when the time and the space seemed right. Everything seemed right on the first Sunday of 1983. To anyone who roamed around the Wisconsin countryside, he reasoned, the Chief's words were still appropriate, still full of meaning.

I agreed. For even as Ron Leys talked, Chief Seattle's words seemed to burst from the pages like living things:

> Teach your children what we have taught our children, that the Earth is our mother. Whatever befalls the Earth befalls the sons of the Earth. If men spit upon the ground, they spit upon themselves. Man belongs to the Earth. All things are connected like the blood which united one family.
>
> Man did not weave the web of life; he is merely a strand in it. Whatever he does to the web, he does to himself.

A lot of people don't want to be reading that in the outdoor section. They want to be reading about hunting and fishing and snowmobiling.

You start printing stuff by dead Indians in your newspaper and your telephones will light up like a call-in show. On abortion.

> Even here, said the Sioux medicine man John Fire Lame Deer, in South Dakota: we are conscious that somewhere out in those hills there are missile silos and radar stations. White men always pick the few unspoiled, beautiful, awesome spots for the sites of these abominations. You have raped and violated these lands, always saying, "Gimme, gimme, gimme," and never giving anything back. You have taken 200,000 acres of our Pine Ridge reservation and made them into a bombing range. This land is so beautiful and strange that now some of you want to make it into a national park. The only use you have made of this land since you took it from us was to blow it up. You have not only despoiled the earth, the rocks, the minerals, all of which you call dead but which are very much alive; you have even changed the animals, which are part

of us, part of the Great Spirit, changed them in a horrible way so no one can recognize them. There is power in a buffalo—spiritual magical power—but there is no power in an Angus, in a Hereford. . . .

From the days of the earliest treaties, Vine Deloria, Jr. has noted, Indians were shocked at the white man's attitude toward land. The tribal elders laughed contemptuously at the idea that a man could sell land.

"Why not sell the air we breathe, the water we drink, the animals we hunt?"

It seemed ludicrous to Indians that people would consider land as a commodity that could be owned by one man. The land, they would answer, supports all life. It is given to all people. No one has a superior claim to exclusive use of land, much less does anyone have the right to fence off a portion and deny others its use.

As Chief Seattle told the President's man:

When the last red man shall have perished, and the memory of my tribe shall have become a myth among the white man, these shores will swarm with the invisible dead of my tribe, and when your children's children think themselves alone in the field, the store, the shop or in the silence of the pathless woods, they will not be alone. . . . So, if we sell you our land, love it as we have loved it. Care for it as we have cared for it. . . .

That's why the outdoor editor draws heat in Milwaukee, and would in *any city* you'd care to name. That's why the phones light up.

ONE FAMILY

Martha

"**I** so regard myself as one of the 'Last of the Pioneer Ladies,' " Martha Gutensohn was saying, "partly because of where I was born and partly because of where I lived later."

Martha is my mother-in-law. We were just sitting around yesterday, drinking coffee and talking. It was her eighty-second birthday.

She spent her first five years in Port Washington, Ohio, where "the big events were the gypsies and the tramps coming through." Her father was a Moravian minister here and they had a horse and surrey "to see the neighbors." They also had the Ohio Canal for skating when it was cold enough.

In 1902, the family moved to Ephraim, Wisconsin, and Martha's sister, Katharine, remains in Door County to this day, a lifelong resident of Sturgeon Bay.

In the autumn of 1902, Martha recalls, there was only one summer cottage in all of Ephraim, no hotels, and she doubts if there were "a hundred people" in the whole countryside. That was the year they started building the first structure of what would eventually become the Anderson Hotel.

169

"It was a wonderful place for a child," she says. "The beach was as free as the air. Life was primitive. The parsonage was next to the Anderson Hotel and we shared a two-handled pump for water between us."

They had a wood stove. An outdoor privy.

"I didn't have an inside toilet," she laughs, "until I got to Colorado. That was in 1923. I was twenty-six then."

She was married by then, to a young man named Sam, who was also a minister. As a matter of fact, their only son became a minister—"for a little while"—before he wound up in Massachusetts state government.

Her life with Sam took them to parsonages in North Dakota, Colorado, Missouri, Iowa and Wisconsin. After Sam died in 1950—"almost thirty years ago—and that's longer than we were married"—she went back to teaching school for another fifteen years.

Despite all those ministers in the family she doesn't think of herself as a "religious" person.

"I'm not pious," she insists. "All those years have given me a strong, basic faith in Life. In People. And in the Possibility of Good."

She thinks she was influenced more by Ephraim than any other place.

"The people there," she says, "gave you a feeling of love and a real desire for education."

But Colorado left a profound impression too.

"On the Western Slope in the 1920s," she remembers, "Sam and I met people who were fleeced in a land scheme and they stayed right there and put their lives together. They had lost all their money and yet they stayed and worked it out."

The lesson of Colorado was: When hardship comes, meet it head on. *It will make you stronger.*

Martha has come from the pioneer life to boarding jets to visit her scattered children. And ten grandchildren. She doesn't presume to advise any of them.

"I think it's tougher for young people to grow up today than it was so long ago in Ephraim. And having made so many mistakes in my own life, I say only this to young people: Make your own mistakes, but don't let those mistakes get you down."

She sits erect, her hands folded, like every teacher you've ever known.

"I also tell them," she says primly, "that I've learned not to worry because the things that you worry about don't happen. Other things happen."

Helen

"Ah," the poet asks, "what is so rare as a day in spring?" "Ah, indeed," Steady Eddy responds, "the answer to the question is: That very spring day in the month of December."

Yesterday was that kind of day, an Indian Spring day, Steady calls it, when you're tempted to watch the sky for geese going north and the geese are almost tempted to go.

A sneaky kind of day, sunny and blue and so warm with little breezes you start expecting crocus on the southern slope.

A gift from God, this day.

Helen's birthday.

I brewed up a cup of Red Zinger tea and took it out in the backyard, the backyard battened down for heavy weather.

Alongside the house, the Blue Canoe was beddy-bye, bottom up and settled down for a long winter's nap.

Under the naked oaks, the Koenig feeder was full to the gunwhales with plump sunflower seeds designed to keep the wintering cardinals likewise.

The picnic table was swept clean, the only placesetting some stones from Little Sister Bay.

And yet Winter wasn't today.

Today was sleepy sunlight and sweet wind and Helen's birthday.

I remembered the summer day she gathered them and there was Vince picking up others on the short hop and making the long throw to first out in the bay.

I remembered the early morning Vince came into this world and his sisters before him.

I remembered the time when I thought marrying a minister's daughter, a Preacher's Kid, was a pretty straight, unrevolutionary thing to do. Later events, however, have proved that I've been hanging out with the most political person since Madame DeFarge.

"Some persons," Steady points out, "tend to their knitting that way."

In a day and age when you can clock most marriages with an egg timer, it's a pleasure to recall that we've been married forever and she says I'm still her friend.

It's also a pleasure to recall that she's taught me all there is to know about a relationship:

Number One: Marriage is Something you go through with Somebody.

Number Two: Home is a place, where, when you have to go there, they have to take you in. She says Robert Frost said that first, but he said it for everybody, particularly the next line in the poem *The Death of the Hired Man*: I should have called it (home) something you somehow haven't to deserve.

On her birthday, you can't get her another Pete Seeger album because she must have every one he's ever recorded.

You can't get her another friend either, because everyone she meets becomes one.

Out here in the Winter Springtime, I wish I could give her this day.

She would promptly share it with her friends, Steady says. "Just give her all the days you got left," he advises, "only save a couple for catfishing."

So be it. Happy Birthday.

Friend.

Christmas Tree

You walk our neighborhood these holiday evenings and everybody has the Christmas trees and Chanukah bushes up and glowing and then you come to our house and the tree is still in the carport.

It's like that every year and I, for one, kind of like it this way.

True, our Christmas tree is always the very last one to get put up. But it's also the very last one to get taken down. Steady

Eddy always says that you can't just turn the Holiday Season like a switch, you have to work up to it, so we work up to it.

"It kills me," Steady says, "to see a Christmas tree thrown out on December 26th. Or for that matter, January 26th."

Me too. In our childhood neighborhood, more than one tree made it to March and in some households until the start of baseball season, albeit by then, bald as coat racks. Jo and Vince cut our tree at Kellman's again this year and it's a full bodied little beauty. It leans against the carport wall casually in no hurry to come inside, like an actor in the wings, awaiting the onstage cue.

The tree is dark and its lifeblood is congealing and it seems a shame to kill a tree for one day.

"Or a trout. Or a turkey," Steady observes. "Geez, you hang out with thinkers, you could wind up eating stone soup."

I thought about the living pines on the warm summer days when the fragrance of hemlock hangs in the air like wine and the forest floor is a coppery soft carpet.

The needles fall, Aldo Leopold had written, and are filed in the duff to enrich the wisdom of the stand. It is this accumulated wisdom that hushes the footsteps of whoever walks under pines.

Even as I peeked at our Christmas tree in the carport, a fox sparrow flew in, alighted on a branch and sat motionless as an ornament. Only a cardinal would have been sweeter. And sadder.

It was in midwinter, Aldo had said, that he sometimes gleaned from his pines something more important than woodlot politics and the news of wind and weather. This was especially likely to happen on some gloomy evening when the snow had buried all irrelevant detail, and the hush of elemental sadness lay heavy upon every living thing. Nevertheless, his pines, each with a burden of snow, were standing ramrod-straight, rank upon rank, and in the dusk beyond, he could sense the presence of hundreds more.

"At such times," Aldo said, "I feel a curious transfusion of courage."

I watched the sparrow in the tree for I don't know how long and for a while, I was seriously figuring on how to get both of them into the house, the bird and the tree.

173

I fixed a cup of tea, hung out with the fireplace for a spell and waited a decent interval.

When I went back to the tree, the sparrow was gone.

Family Christmas

We normally don't go for a walk on Christmas Day.

We normally sit inside by the fire sipping hot wine or mulled cider and pass the afternoon in conversation until it's time for dinner. Then we sip hot wine or mulled cider and pass the evening in conversation.

But this Christmas was different.

First, Donna and Martha walked the Hoyt Park area and the bluffs where they grew up.

They got back just as Vince and I were about to head out the other way and Martha decided to walk with us too.

We walked three abreast down to the Arboretum.

Then single-file across the frozen marshes.

I remembered all those snowy years of following in my father's footsteps and now I was following in my kids' footsteps and it seemed like I had spent my whole life bringing up the rear.

This bohunk family had produced its share of leaders, and by damn, I had followed them all.

We moved onto the frozen surface of Wingra and headed down the shoreline to the left.

The lake stretched away like a desert. The powder snow glistened in a sea of mica. We strung out and walked toward the knot of people clustered around the gaily painted boxsled.

The Magical Mystery Tour Sled! Belonging to the One and Only, Vince Colletti.

And there he was, not actually fishing himself, but rather instructing two young men in the Art of Actual Fishing.

He took the jigging pole from one.

"Not your whole arm," Colletti snapped. "Just your wrist. See."

He held the pole like a baton. A wand. And flicked it in a fluid movement.

"Have to teach them," he said. "Or they don't catch nothin'."

Later as we walked off the lake, young Vince asked me if old Vince was related to the young men and I told him I didn't think so, but it didn't make any difference, the whole world was Colletti's family.

We cut across the lagoon, paid a courtesy call on the Herbsts, where Jurgen had the Battle of Smolensk spread out on a card table, and walked west on the railroad tracks.

The kids wanted to shortcut through the cemetery and so we did, crunching through the clean stillness, the crows low flying and fleeing without fear, the dark living pines looking down on the bright artificial flowers.

We detoured to the grave of our great friend Cedric Parker, buried here only last Spring.

The sheltering tree was leafless, the snowfield unbroken, the silence thundering with memories.

For a moment, it was as if we were at the grave of our other great friend far to the north, The Old Man sleeping in another unbroken snowfield. We stood there, silently, and I thanked them both for sending us Colletti.

The Old Professionals

*I*n the cozy bait shop the other day, Steady Eddy was rigging tipups: One for northern. One for walleye. The Old Pro doing it, he called it.

"You know," he said, spooling on line, "when people meet me for the first time they're shocked, because they always thought I was in my sixties."

I told him it was because he said wise things. And most people figured only Old Professionals said Wise Things.

That got us onto Charlie Bran and Lew Cornelius, a couple of Old Professionals if ever there were any, a couple of legends even while they lived.

Lew Cornelius had loved baseball, and when he managed the Monona Grove Lakers, he always wound up with the best players in the area on his teams. The Richters. The Bakkens.

The players. Steady, who knew Lew on and off the ball field, could probably do a book on the Ole Sarge.

"I pitched for Lew one season," Steady said, "and he just *loved* practice. I don't mean he loved to run the practice. I mean he used to love to *watch* it."

Steady said Lew would stand out behind the mound just watching everything and talking to the pitcher and "not manage."

"One time it rained," Steady said, "and everybody left the field except Lew. He just stood there, looking up, getting soaked. He really hated to leave a ball diamond, no matter what."

It came to me that even though he is gone now, Lew hasn't really left the ball diamond, because they'll never stop playing that game. He's probably out there behind that pitcher's mound, waiting. Looking up.

It also came to me that Lew had brilliant teams, yet not too many people ever accused the manager of being brilliant. But it must have been that, when it looked like he wasn't really managing, he was really managing. When you watch something with love, the guru says, you are watching with "soft eyes."

Day in and day out, Charlie Bran was probably the best fisherman the Madison lakes have ever seen—or ever will. You'd see Charlie in all kinds of weather, in all kinds of water, with all kinds of fish. He was Merlin with a magic wand, materializing fish out of places where no one else could. On the locks. The breakwaters. The open lakes.

"Just *watching* him," Russ said a lifetime ago on Mendota, "is like attending a clinic."

I don't know if Lew Cornelius and Charlie Bran knew each other well or at all, but the way Steady was linking them drove me to read again the Chinese poet Hsu Chi, dead these 700 years.

> The two old men
> Sit in silence together.
> Living in dim memories
> Of the past.
> They are lifelong friends
> And need no words
> To share their thoughts.

One quavers to the other
"May you live a hundred years
And may I live ninety-nine."

The other nods his old white head
and gravely says:
"Let us go home together
And drink a cup of wine."

Mother and Father Himmelsbach

*M*y mother always held the Army of the United States responsible for my losing my religion, in view of the fact that I had it when I entered the Army.

It was Catholicism, and my folks figured that I lost it "somewhere in Europe."

That was partly true. Certainly, the whole process started over there when you got to thinking what a dumb thing it was that people killed each other in a war, and what an even dumber thing that German Catholics, French Catholics, American Catholics, and all the other Catholics could also kill each other in a war. Not to mention Lutherans.

All the different armies had their Catholic chaplains who took care of their respective flocks and blessed their souls and blessed their arms, and then the soldiers made the Sign of the Cross and went out and tried to kill each other.

It put you in a terrible bind.

And if it put you there, where did it put your God, Who was not only processing your marching orders like a company clerk but being cited as the authority who issued them?

It was an aspect of religion that had never come up in the parochial confines of Holy Assumption parish, where you were schooled in all the other aspects.

I remember one of the nuns saying that the most wretched of all was the man "who turned his back on Holy Mother Church." We prayed extra for that man, thankful that we didn't

177

know him and assuming that he lived off somewhere in Wauwatosa or Shorewood or maybe even Whitefish Bay but *thank God*, not in West Allis. We used to like the idea that his ears were burning because so many people were talking about him, and sometimes Charlie Kaiser and I would be walking up Greenfield Avenue and see some old guy rubbing and scratching his ear like there were flies bothering him or mosquitoes and we'd say in a whisper: "That's him! The man who turned his back! Probably just visiting. Waiting for a street car to go home." We'd spray him with some more quiet prayers like a spiritual Flit gun. We wanted to drive him crazy so he would come back to Church and his ears would stop itching.

When I came back from the Army, it was to the North Country. My folks were living on the Big Stone Lake, parishioners of St. Theresa Catholic Church six miles away in Three Lakes. The parish was predominantly Polish, and it was said that the priests had to be bilingual in order to hear the confessions of the old-timers. The priest and pastor then was the Rev. Joseph Himmelsbach.

I got back from the Army in the dead of winter, and in those days before snowmobiles and the ski boom, before television even, dead is what the North Country winter was. Dead and long. Everybody followed the high school basketball team to keep from getting cabin fever, and on Sundays you just naturally came into Three Lakes to get the Milwaukee papers and go to Mass and visit a little. I went to Mass with the folks regularly, and you could tell as Father Himmelsbach faced the congregation and looked us over before he began his sermon and announcements that he was pleased to see so many little family groups there.

You could tell, even from the back, who was a family and who wasn't. Couples who were engaged always sat very straight up and dignified like they didn't even know each other. Families were kind of jammed in close to each other even when there was room to spread out, especially in the wintertime when there were no tourists and the little church was kind of echoey because there weren't enough people there to absorb the sound and make it comforting and homey.

Sometimes Father Himmelsbach would fix you with a stare while he was preaching like he was going to ask questions. That always gave you a twinge, because you weren't always listening closely, or listening at all, and he knew it.

That feeling doesn't happen to you in the big, big churches. There you get the feeling you're practically invisible. There's safety in numbers, or at least the illusion of safety. It's like a school of baitfish, in a huge ball, watching the barracuda, trying not to provide individual targets. That may be why the families huddled together in church.

I went to Mass every Sunday—but no more to Confession or Communion, and I wondered if Father Himmelsbach was wondering about that. I stopped going to Mass when the ice went out and the regular fishing season opened. I spent Sunday mornings on the Chain of Lakes sloughs, alone.

I just never managed to be back by the time the folks left for church. That's when my mother started blaming the Army of the United States. It was kind of funny, because she was not Catholic to begin with and had converted. My father, who *had* been Catholic to begin with, didn't blame the Army of the United States or anyone. Old fishermen, I've learned, tend to be less judgmental, more philosophical about fish they lose.

Father Himmelsbach began to drop in on us regularly, and we'd talk, and he'd say, "I missed you at Mass Sunday." The first few times I made excuses, and I really don't know if I made them for him or for me, or maybe for my mother.

I finally told him the reason I didn't go to church anymore was that when I was in church, the birds were on the other side of the stained glass windows, the pine forest was outside the church walls, the sky was above the vaulted ceiling. Everything I saw was *man-made*. It was a man-made box.

In the sloughs, I told Father Himmelsbach, I saw nothing that was man-made except the boat under my feet and the fishing rod in my hand, and I mostly watched and listened and felt very close to God out there.

He didn't scream or shout or show scorn. He smiled. Then he said we had to go fishing sometime. We never did, and every May when the families don't huddle together any more, I remember him. He's gone now, and the new church is brick. I was in it once. For my father's funeral.

The Last Dance

We buried my Uncle George Foale up in Peshtigo the other day. He and his lady friend were dancing at a big fiftieth wedding anniversary party when he said he had to sit down because he was having some difficulty catching his breath. He lost consciousness and his friends couldn't revive him. He was seventy-eight years old.

Uncle George went the way everybody always says they want to go. Dancing. Doing the polka. Doing whatever else you love to do. Fishing a dry fly on the Peshtigo River. Bowling. Birdwatching.

Anything that gets you out and moving around and smiling at people who are doing the same thing.

Anything that keeps you active and toned and not just sitting there like a chipmunk on the patio, absolutely petrified, immobilized in the presence of the resident housecat who then proceeds to toy with you.

Uncle George was one of the active ones. He danced. He fished his beloved walleyes below the dam at Marinette. He loved to tell stories, to flirt with the ladies, pour a few shots for the men, including the parish priest. He'd just bought a brand new Bonneville, with wire wheels, that he called "my baby."

It was his *real* baby, his only child, Dolly, who saved him for dancing and fishing when he was as immobilized as that chipmunk under the cat's paw.

Seven years ago, Uncle George was practically paralyzed from the neck down. The doctors up there diagnosed his condition as Guillain-Barre syndrome—the so-called "French polio." The doctors also said they couldn't do anything for him, that his condition was hopeless and that he should accept that.

His wife accepted the doctors' verdict, and Dolly says her father did, too—figuring, she thinks, that if all these people were saying the same thing they must be right, and who was he to question them?

There was even talk of putting him in a nursing home so he could have round-the-clock professional care. Only one person didn't really accept that.

Dolly.

"I knew my father," she says. "He was a bull and he was a fighter. But he had to believe it was worth fighting for."

Dolly talked her father into trying Sacred Heart Hospital in Milwaukee. They had therapy programs there—tough physical therapy that she thought would help him.

He went, but as Dolly recalls, "he wasn't too enthused."

It was the hospital's policy to accept therapy patients only on probation. It was understood that if after four weeks the staff felt the patient wasn't going to benefit from treatment, they would recommend that the patient go elsewhere.

"It's a life-or-death program for the patient," Dolly says. "You either try or you die. If you don't try, the hospital is saying, you have to go someplace else to die because we need this space for someone who will try."

A therapist practically said that verbatim to Uncle George in an encounter that changed and saved—his life.

"She was a black woman," Dolly recalls, "and she came on strong. She told my father he would probably hate her before they were done, but he could walk out of there on his own. Or he could just leave now. She really got to him. After that he never stopped trying.

In three months he walked out on his own, and everybody in the place said goodbye to him, because by then he knew everyone and everyone knew him.

◦　◦　◦

"George was a fisherman," Father Ralph Merkatoris said at the funeral Mass, "and he has left us now, on this shore.

"It is like watching a sailboat from this shore going to Chambers Island. It is going away from us. We keep watching and it keeps getting smaller, and then it is gone. It has gone away from us.

"But to the people standing on Chambers Island, the sailboat is coming toward them. It keeps getting bigger and bigger. And right now George's wife, Bobbie, and all his fishing friends are standing on that far shore, welcoming him."

Father Merkatoris drove up from Denmark, Wisconsin, to officiate at Uncle George's funeral. Before he was transferred to Holy Trinity of Pine Grove he'd been at St. Mary's. George, the retired plumber-steamfitter—"Praise God"—lived just down the street from the church and its school.

"George would come over in the middle of the night," Father Merkatoris said, "and fix whatever needed to be fixed— the plumbing, the heating. Then he would invite you over to the house for a couple of shots. He loved people. He loved to help them."

✼ ✼ ✼

After the funeral, and the meal in the school cafeteria, and the visiting, we drove up to Marinette to see the place below the dam where Uncle George fished his beloved wall-eyes.

There were a half-dozen gates open, and the water boiled through wild as the *dalles* of the Wolf.

One fisherman, an old pro with a pencil mustache, was packing up on the street. He had one walleye. Respectable.

He said this was great walleye water. He was retired, and he spent seven months of the year up here, fishing this water, living out of his camper. He asked if we lived here or were just passing through. I said we were up for my uncle's funeral. George Foale in Peshtigo.

"George?" he said. "Was he a retired plumber? George from Peshtigo? Sure, I fished with him. Everybody knows George."

He was surprised George was dead. He wasn't surprised that he died dancing. He said his name was Garland Buckley. He said he would pass the word.

The Old Man

We were sitting on my mother's front porch at the little house on Big Stone Lake, and I was just kind of thinking about The Old Man because he used to spend a lot of time sitting there when he wasn't out chasing grouse or walleyes or dreaming up some project that was bound to improve the Old Place one day.

I used to think that his projects were dreamed up to specifically improve my back muscles because an awful lot of them involved a shovel or a bucksaw or an axe and usually me, dragooned into physical work that always, *always* seemed so absurdly monumental at the outset that I secretly prayed he couldn't pull it off.

But he always did.

There was the time he decided that we were going to cut down every popple tree within reaching distance of the house, and we not only did that, we kept on going, and after we were done cutting, the nearest standing popple was in the Nicolet National Forest in a roofless area.

God, we went through those trees like a couple of berserk beavers. It *must* have been dozens and dozens (it might as well have been hundreds and hundreds) of watery, core-rotted trees, and I can still feel the pain of them cutting into my shoulders as we carried them off the battlefield.

Looking back, it may not have been *monumental*, but it was done before the chainsaw appeared in the north woods; it was done by hand, and that's as prideful as building a pyramid.

There was the time he decided that we were going to fill in the low land behind the cottages with sand, and that made the basement dig look like a Tonka project. We dug out a canyon you wouldn't believe, filling Johnny Kotarski's dump truck, and we dug out the dump truck more than once before the project was done.

I sit on the porch where The Old Man used to sit, and I remember the blisters, the calluses, the sheer agony of what I used to think was mind-numbing labor. I remember, too, The Old Man's valiant attempts to get through to me.

Hard work never killed anybody, I hear him saying yet, and then twinkling. *Well, maybe a couple of people.*

I smile at that now, as I never smiled at it then, and there is a flurry of activity as the hummingbirds come to the liquid feeders outside the porch window.

My wife got my mother the first feeder, and it was so successful that my mother had to get a second one so the hummingbirds wouldn't bunch up and fight so much.

Not including the grandchildren, that feeder might just be the best present we ever gave Mom; maybe even including the grandchildren.

183

Flights of ruby-throated hummingbirds homed in on the extended feeding tube like minature fighter planes converging on an aerial tanker.

They zoomed around windows like some kind of Flying Circus. They had crazy moves, not all smoothly arcing poetry, but fits and starts like sewing machine stitches, short, herky-jerky, straight-line moves that resembled zippers opening and closing.

I don't recall that we ever had hummingbirds around in the old days, and here's my mother saying that everybody she knows up here has hummingbirds now because they all feed them. Only she has more hummingbirds than anyone else.

"I think," she says, "it's because of that tree."

That tree is a balsam, almost as high as the house.

I remember vividly the day The Old Man planted it. Here's a house, surrounded by a pine forest, and he's planting another tree in the front yard.

I don't know why he planted it there.

But there isn't another balsam for blocks around, and you can see how the hummingbirds use the security blanket of the spreading branches as some sort of Advance Base. They zip in and out of the greenery, busy as bees, chasing and being chased, the little wings a blur, their little bodies burning up energy like there's no tomorrow. And they don't seem to give a care because they know where there's plenty more.

I'm not saying The Old Man planted that tree for the little birds who would visit his wife faithfully every year after he was gone. What I'm saying is: *It wouldn't surprise me none.*

The Old Man's Garage

I got to thinking just now about the deer head hanging in The Old Man's garage. Actually, it's my mother's garage, but habit dies hard. I still call it his because it was always packed with his stuff.

He always had so much stuff in there, the car often sat outside under the pines. Even when he put an addition onto the garage, his stuff just sort of accumulated and expanded to fit the space and the car was a real tight squeeze again.

It was your typical North Country inventory: a workbench that ran the length of one wall, overflowing with pails of nails and screws, nuts and bolts, pliers, hammers, chisels, wrenches, and all the tools you ever needed to drill a well or put in plumbing or wire a house or pour concrete or saw up logs or weld or paint or catch fish or butcher deer.

It was The Old Man's garage and not the big house next to it that contained The Old Man's lifestyle, that contained his essence, that contained his spirit.

From canepoles to Coleman lanterns, from outboard motors to shotgun shells, from icefishing tipups to rain ponchos, that endless clutter drew me like a magnet. I spent countless hours poking around in there, amazed at what I discovered, because what I discovered was The Old Man.

He's gone now, and his clutter is gone, too—most of it to friends and neighbors who could use it, some of it squirreled away in my den at home—and the garage is so neat and unlived-in that he wouldn't recognize it.

The deer head is still there, though—it even got to hang in the summer porch of the big house for a time—and it watches over the cold, lifeless garage with its cold, lifeless eyes.

A trophy, Aldo Leopold tried to teach us in *A Sand County Almanac*, whether it be a bird's egg, a mess of trout, a basket of mushrooms, the photograph of a bear, the pressed specimen of a wildflower or a note tucked into the cairn on a mountain peak, is a certificate.

"It attests," Aldo said, "that its owner has been somewhere and done something—exercised skill, persistence or discrimination in the age-old feat of overcoming, outwitting or reducing-to possession. These connotations which attach to the trophy usually far exceed its physical value."

I have only to close my eyes and here I am, up there in The Old Man's garage, the concrete clean-swept, the workbench neat and empty because no one works there anymore, the car gone to Florida for the winter.

There we are, just the two of us in this place.

I stare up at the trophy buck.

The trophy buck stares down at me.

Do we comprehend each other? We are each of us strange artifacts of another time, another life.

I remember driving the cedar swamp with The Old Man in that other time, in that other life.

* * *

Across the snow filled valley land
our father watches from his stand.
Here, our big buck cleared the stream.
The damning prints in the frozen sand.

Upwind, we work as a combat team.
An army of cedars waits in the steam
between us now and our father's place.
Through 7× glasses, he sees an old dream.

Remember the flush on a young man's face
the first time he opened his rifle case?
In this swamp, one great last deer.
Listening for drivers, gauging our pace.

He knows again that we are near.
It is the terrible time of year.
The others hope we find him here.
I hope we do not find him here.

* * *

In Dostoevski's *The Brothers Karamazov*, the monk, on his deathbed, admonishes his followers: "Love all the earth, every ray of God's light, every grain of sand or blade of grass, every living thing. If you love the earth enough, you will know the divine mystery."

Amen. The rest is taxidermy.

Poem for the Old Man

It snowed today, starting early, a Christmas kind of snow in the month of March. By midmorning, the words no longer came, the writing freezing up like the creeks outside.

I built the fire up, swept my little corner clean, put a pot of chili on, got the kettle going good for tea.

❉

It was this kind of day
that had been The Old Man's last
in that terrible hospital bed.
Shrunken, shriveled,
all the Light leaving him
Like a fire that has
nowhere to go because
there's nothing left to burn
In that small North Country bed
that small body was my father.
My God. My God.
Where did the rest of him go?

❉

It came to me then that some of him had gone into me.
In the mirror, I even saw parts of him there for the very first
time. *That is your nose,* I said out loud. *Man, that is really your
nose.* As a matter of fact, that is really your face. What is happening here? We are no more father and son. We are brother
and brother.

❉

My father would take us
for the fish.
On the U.S. Government pier,
foreigners thick
as the Green Bay flies.
They had their trolley lines
for the perch.
We carried the bait
and the galvanized pails.
Waiting, we watched
the young men diving.
They went like rocks, like stones.
My father on the great stone wall.
Looking and looking
and tending his lines.

There was a baker called Vogel
who fished with my father
and drank like a fish

my father said.
They knew the lakes
around Milwaukee.
Pewaukee, Tichigan and
the treacherous Wind.
In Spring, they drove North
and followed the walleyes
into the Wolf.
In the New London nights,
the taste of snow
and heavy fish
sagging with spawn.
Big Lake Winnebago breaking up in the dark.
The German baker
shaping his dreams
in baking pans.
His life measured out:
Fifths and pints and poppyseed.
My father told me once, no more:
Louie Vogl afraid of Tomorrow.
He lost *something*, my father said.
What it was, he would not say.
One day, the baker
in his basement
hung from the soilpipe by his belt.
That was the Winter.
The very next Spring
The Old Man and me.
On the Wolf River
for walleyes.
The crows are coming
to clean our woods.
Beneath their wings,
a littered world waits.
The snowfield
like some frozen surf
Releases dead things to the sun:
Little bodies and bits of fur
Dead these hundred days and more.
The French called it

Butte des Morts
Hill of the Dead.
We mourn them too.

❀

When I was young, I spent this kind of morning in church.
This kind and every other kind, too.
Walled-in we were in those days. The sun was shut out.
We lighted the candles and waited for Something to happen. Now we are not walled in that way anymore.
We walk the woods on this kind of morning and nothing more has to happen at all.

❀

The whole day went that way, funny, not really lazy, funny kind of day. Snowing, cooking chili, didn't do much. Straightened up my little hutch. Just sort of hung out with The Old Man. I even lit a candle for him. It wasn't sad or anything.
It was a green bayberry.
It made everything smell
like Christmas.

The Prof Leads the Way

*H*arold Jordahl—The Prof to his students and just Bud to his friends—and I spent the other day at his farm tucked away in the coulee country of Richland County.

On the face of it, we were there to do some trouting, for these hills hide the silver little waters that hide the silver little fish. But along the way, we spent a lot of the sun-sweetened day tramping the ridges, poking around in the valleys and performing all those soul-satisfying activities Bud calls "researching the project."

And this land—the challenge of managing this land—has become Bud's project.

No—more than that. This land has become his life's work.

189

In his chino pants and work boots, a bottle of beer in his tanned hand, he could pass for your average game warden. Or forest ranger. Or farmer.

He's proud of that, because he understands these folks and their problems. He's one of them.

But the moment he starts talking, you know you're hanging out with a pretty rare bird indeed.

His background was essentially forestry, but he felt he had to broaden himself beyond a single specialty, because to work with Nature, to "manage" Nature (and he says to use that word advisedly, because you don't really *manage* Nature), you find out what Ma Nature's House Rules and Regulations are, and then you kind of "caretake" while Ma manages herself.

"The trouble with specialties," Bud says as a former specialist, "is that you literally can't see the forest for the trees. One person is an expert on bugs, another on trees, another on soil, another on water, another on air, and on and on. But the only way to understand Nature and how she works is to collate, if you will, *all the specialties into one discipline, one holistic study.* That's Ecology, and that's what we need desperately."

Bud squinted at the once-gullied hills, now knit whole and healthy by the healing alfalfa, and I was struck by how much he was beginning to look like Aldo Leopold and sound like Sigurd Olson. I was struck, too, by how much the words he was speaking now reminded me of the words written by Stephen Levine in his book, *Planet Steward: Journal of a Wildlife Sanctuary*:

> I begin to learn the ten thousand forms that have arisen from the One: names, shapes, properties, divinities, histories; how the soil came about, the different kinds of rock, the fossil pollens of plants that have preceded this voyager man by many eons; the calls of dozens of species; the tracks of carnivores, angels and wood nymphs, the dihedral sweep of the vulture, planet janitor; porcupine's nibblings as telltale signs; fox, badger, skunk, coyote; and heavy-handed self-justifying man—the greatest of predators, the only saint.

We drive the ridge to the fishing water, and Bud points into the lush valley far below.

Three deer graze the alfalfa, round-rumped and sleek as horses.

We pass the drumming log where, last time, we watched the motionless grouse for an eternity. And he watched us.

We drop down into the fishing valley and park, and when we alight, two red-tailed hawks hang high on the thermal, a living mandala of the sacred places.

The Planet Steward had written:

Each being here is the mother and sacrifice of every other. There is none that is not a perfect part of the whole. Each creature is indispensable, rising and falling in its time for the furtherance of every other creature. This is place of breeding and feeding. The owl chants the night. Dove Orpheus coos up the moon. The flycatchers, titmice, grosbeaks, ravens, hawks, woodpeckers, eagles, vultures, sparrows, swifts, chats, mockingbirds, bluebirds and hummingbirds are strophe to the antistrophe of the crickets, beetles, fireflies, scarlet dragonflies and the multi-formed crawlings of the moist unknowns. The turtle, algae on his shell, moves like a Zen garden across the duckweed. The native fish find dark cathedral in the winding stream. This is the planet brotherhood.

We take our rods and Bud leads the way.

He stops and stands over a rock-rimmed springhole. Then he points to a rectangular depression in the forest floor above it.

"Folks lived here," Bud says. "A hundred years ago. They farmed here, using this water, this spring. Probably ran it down to the tank below for the stock. That's the old town road along the treeline."

The old town road, like the old house site, was an overgrown depression in the forest floor.

I thought of how it must have been for those people in this place a hundred years ago, and the hawks watching.

"They probably planted those trees along the old road," Bud said. "They left two trees."

Not much, maybe, but most of us don't leave even that.

Then we went fishing.

The Man Called Levelwind

They got to be a pretty blase bunch around the baitshop, not much given to wild demonstrations for either causes or candidates or what the world outside calls *champions*.

"We are not," Steady Eddy, the proprietor, has declared on more than one festive night, "your average groupies."

True, the baitshop continues to be impressed by the accomplishments of an Eric Heiden, or a Henry Aaron, or a Robin Yount. But the list is as short as summer at Great Bear Lake.

At the baitshop, every champion in the world takes a backseat to the man they call *Levelwind*.

"When you say Levelwind," Steady says, "you've said it all."

Dave Johnson is the man they call Levelwind. He used to live in Madison, now in Minnesota, and a couple of years back had the kind of championship season that becomes the stuff of legend.

In that one miraculous winter, Dave Johnson hauled out more large walleye pike from Lake Mendota than anybody living has ever heard of.

Six-pound walleyes. Seven-pound walleyes. Eight-pound walleyes. Nine-pound walleyes. By that time, he was attracting bigger crowds than the metal detectors at O'Hare, and despite that, one memorable day he pulled out a golden winter walleye weighing ten pounds.

"He was on the greatest roll I've ever seen," Steady says in awe, and one assumes that as an ex-paratrooper, Steady has witnessed the great rolls that clean you out and put you on the pad to boot. "If it had been in Vegas, he would own the casino."

When I stopped at the baitshop last week, there was Dave Johnson, like a visiting firefighter checking out the local department.

Levelwind said he missed the Madison lakes, especially Mendota, even though he now lived within a few minutes' drive of four lakes that were "pretty good."

His job selling aluminum window and door frames to architects and builders brings him into Madison every month or so, and he likes to touch base with Steady Eddy. It was Steady, after all, who, when they were spooling braided line onto a tipup one day, noticed the meticulous way Dave got the line to lie flat by tilting and tipping the spool.

"Just like a levelwind reel," Steady says.

Steady likes to look for nicknames. When he saw that, he stopped looking. That's what you do for friends.

In a way, it's surprising that they're still speaking, let alone friends. Considering what Steady Eddy did to Levelwind, you would have expected Levelwind to do something to Steady. Like bulldozing the baitshop to the ground.

"Or at the very least," says Hugo Willie, "towing it out to the Brearly Street bar."

What Steady Eddy did to Levelwind happened during that championship walleye season.

"Anybody who asked where the walleyes were hitting," Steady admits, "I'd tell them to fish off Second Point. Look for the guy in the orange snowmobile suit fishing tipups."

"They found me," Levelwind says. "Geez, guys were drilling holes right next to my boots. It looked like an oilfield out there. I thought we were gonna sink."

He changed snowmobile suits, from blaze orange to a less flamboyant black.

Steady changed with the times.

"I told them to look for the guy," he confesses, "in the black snowmobile suit fishing tipups."

"You wouldn't believe the gang out there," Levelwind says. "People were coming from Chicago."

The people coming from Chicago were as much Levelwind's fault as they were Steady's.

In February, Steady's friend John Spehn, the outdoors writer for the *Chicago Sun-Times*, came up to fish walleyes on Mendota in the custody of Steady and of course, Dave Levelwind Johnson.

The good news was that they caught five walleyes between two and six pounds, and lost two more "that went eight pounds each."

The bad news, as far as Levelwind was concerned, was that John Spehn printed the whole account in the *Sun-Times*.

"The phone rang off the wall," Steady marvels. "Guys wanted to come up and fish walleyes with 'Levelwind.' "

He fishes walleyes the way most people fish perch. Move that bait. A foot off bottom. Eight feet. Twelve feet. But standing next to him is no guarantee. Paul Zoch, who was one of Charlie Bran's buddies, was with Levelwind once, and before he got his tipups set, Levelwind had two big walleyes flopping on the ice.

"I grew up out there," Levelwind says of frozen Lake Mendota. "As a kid, I'd walk from home with my gear and fish all winter long."

His schoolboy schedule carried over into adulthood. He'd be off Second Point around three in the afternoon, fish, and be off the ice at six-thirty.

His preference for solitude also carried over. "He's a loner," Steady confirms. "Absolutely."

That championship season was his last year in Madison, and it was a rough one. His marriage was on the rocks and would end in divorce. Chapters were closing in his life. He would have to leave Madison. . . . It was as if Nature herself were comforting this loner, this lifetime friend. Maybe that's the real secret.

Everybody that year was out there looking for walleyes. That year Levelwind was out there looking for something else.

Nick and a Taste for Fishing

*T*here are those who require traditional proofs before they will accept the fact that Spring has indeed arrived and no mistake.

Some folks won't believe until the sky is dark with wedges of Canada geese going north, their bugling joyful as hounds scattering rabbits to all points of the compass.

Some folks won't believe until that magical night you can watch the Brewers at County Stadium without wearing thermal underwear.

Some folks won't believe until the Mineral Lake Card and Bird Watching Society caucuses in the cookshack and votes on it.

Me? I believe when I bump into Nick Stoneman and he says he's antsy to go fishing.

I bumped into Nick the other day at the supermarket and that's what he said.

Nick, you understand, is in his eighties, but simply doesn't look it. Like George Burns.

"I rubbed elbows with a lot of old people," Nick told me a couple of years back in *Madison* magazine, "and sometimes I wonder what the hell I am still doing here."

In the aisle at the market, I told him that he looked good.

He got that crafty catcher's look he gets when he's onto something and comes up out of the crouch, firing.

"There are three stages to a man's life," he said. "Young, Old and 'Gee, you look good.' "

A lot of troutwater has gone under the bridge since Nick retired from Badger Sporting Goods, the firm he founded with Allie Vilberg back in 1941.

"My wife Madeline," Nick notes, "says, 'You retired too soon and we're living too long.' "

> *The prairie lands begin to dry.*
> *The pastures fill with dairy herds.*
> *It is a time to be reborn.*
> *For the young a buddy, a hat, a ball.*
> *For the old, a trip again to the River Brule*
> *It is the season of tender things.*
> *Spider rings and silky wings.*
> *Shoots and roots and birthday suits.*
> *Colts and calves. Kittens, pups.*
> *Budding fields and buttercups.*
> *Slow sun marshes.*
> *Fast cold streams.*
> *The Old Man waits*
> *with his young man dreams.*

He played baseball with Dynie Mansfield on the old Madison Blues, and he fished with Dynie as much as anyone. Buddies they were, poking in the Wisconsin backwaters like Butch and Sundance, Tom and Huck, Robin and Little John.

Fishing buddies are a breed apart, as Gordon MacQuarrie noted when he described one of his—who also happened to be his father-in-law—in *Stories of the Old Duck Hunters and Other Drivel*:

> It made me shiver just to look at that part of the Brule. We were down below Armstead's farm, north of the town of Brule. There were snowy patches in the hollows, the day was gray, and from the lake blew a searching cold.
>
> The Rt. Hon. President was lively as a cricket. He had buckled into waders while I was pulling on extra socks—reluctantly. For him the birds were singing and the sun was shining. In him the flame of the zealot burns with a fierce light. He went to the River whistling. . . .

That's Nick Stoneman too—an Old Pro hastening away down the little path on the left bank, embracing the current a hundred yards below. This is duck soup for him. You know about Nick, as MacQuarrie knew about Mr. President, that no shiver is passing through his frame, and you think, disgusted, what frightful fanaticism possesses a man who thus cleaves to his private poison under any conditions.

"I remember how cold I got." MacQuarrie recalls. "I remember how my hands got blue. . . ."

The Old Guys understand dedication like that. Nick tells of the time he and Dynie Mansfield were on the Madison River in Montana—a river they loved so much they "visited" it for over twenty straight summers—and Dynie got into a trout bonanza in the middle of the river with wet flies.

Nick remembers Dynie stayed in that spot like he was nailed to the bottom, catching trout like crazy.

When Dynie finally, finally moved and came off the river, it was the stuff of legend.

"Dynie had a load of trout," Nick said, "and when he pulled off his waders he was all wet. I thought maybe he had shipped water out there, or the waders leaked.

" 'No,' Dynie said. 'That's an *inside* job. With the trout hitting like that, I wasn't about to leave that spot. For *anything.*' "

Nick appreciates that singlemindedness. That's why one of his favorite quotations is from *Fisherman's Bounty*, edited by Nick Lyons.

"You will search far," Sparse Grey Hackle writes, "to find a fisherman who will admit that a taste for fishing, like a taste for liquor, must be governed lest it come to possess its possessor."

"My wife," Nick says, "reminds me of that quotation often."

My wife, too.
Shoots and roots and birthday suits.
Dynie had the leaky boots.

Art and Charlie

*I*t was, as fishing goes, a slow day in the Slough.
True, we were taking the occasional crappie, but the water was not all that warm and the great schools that would eventually throng this place were not in yet.

The minnows, fished patiently in one spot, produced as many crappies as the small jigs, twitched and moved and cast with purpose and then cast with resignation.

"It's like ice fishing," somebody said. "I think they're still too numb to move much."

I remembered being on the ice not too long ago, not too far from here, hunkered down in the snowmobile suit and the Sorel boots, the glacier wind bringing tears to my eyes and blowing the hunting crows back into the far woods, back into silence.

Now the red-winged blackbirds called from the marsh and cardinals marked their territories with that frustrating, unhurried, pouring liquid sound that seemed to be coming from everywhere at once.

"You can trace it right to an empty tree," Steady Eddy says, "and you'd swear the bird was inside. That's spooky."

No, I thought, this isn't like ice fishing at all.

Spring is not Winter. Open water is not frozen water. The marshland stirs with life. This place is pregnant with possibilities.

On the far shore, one male mallard chased another male mallard away from his female companion.

"The original Mona Lisa smile," says Steady, "came from the female mallard."

It's true. It is the wisest, sweetest smile in all of Nature. It's Edith Bunker despite a lifetime with Archie.

Mona and her pugnacious mate moved away to be replaced by another pair of mallards, this time two males. They floated, loose as gooses, without the uptight posturing and possessiveness of Mona's mate. They weren't in any kind of competition; two bachelors, floating and feeding and enjoying the day. Perhaps they had been driven off and out of the spring mating game earlier, or, as Hugo Percy likes to suggest, perhaps they had taken themselves out of the game by choice.

"We're not all psychologically equipped to handle parenting," Perce says. "Maybe your smart ducks got that figured out."

Perce says that just hanging out in the marshes with a good buddy all day long isn't really so dumb. Soaking up the sunshine and the daphnia might add up to a ne'er-do-well duck in some moralist's eyes but Ma Nature doesn't really need or expect *everybody* to contribute to the gene pool.

I watched the two bachelor mallards drifting down that timeless current and I thought of all the old bachelors who had lived in all the old shacks up in the Chain of Lakes country in the timeless past.

I thought of Art and Charlie Brenton, who had lived all those years a short cast from The Old Man's place on Big Stone.

They had been raised downstate, and in the 1940s they were the surviving members of their family, running what used to be called a resort on "the European plan," a few primitive log cabins with inside waterpump and outside privy. I think it was one of the last places on the shore to get electricity, and everybody who had it thought how backward that was. When darkness came, everybody switched on the lights—except the Brentons and their customers, who lit up kerosene lamps. I loved it.

Their little corner of the lake was a little bit of the past, the old North, kerosene lamps and kerosene stoves, woodstoves and wooden boats, oilcloth on the kitchen table and cupboards as distinctively fragrant as the day they were nailed up.

Their little corner of the lake also contained some of the biggest walleyes, and I can recall the nights we trolled back and forth beyond their pier talking to Charlie in the darkness and feeling the walleyes *tap-tap-tapping* the minnow ever so gently.

Charlie loved to talk. He had been "all over" with the Merchant Marine and had an opinion about everything.

I think his brother had an opinion, too, but you never got to hear it because Arthur had "never been anywhere" and was always deferring to Charlie, or listening to Charlie or quoting Charlie when Charlie wasn't there.

Arthur, I guess you'd say now, was a *househusband* before anyone ever knew what that meant. He did the housekeeping, the cleaning, the cooking, and the laundry, and he did it with a quality that made their cabin someplace special.

I loved to stop in there to visit after fishing or hunting or just tramping out in the woods.

Arthur would have a kettle boiling and perhaps some bread baked, or a stew working, and the cabin so clean you'd swear it had been steel-wooled. "Soogied," we used to say in the Merchant Marine.

Some of us used to say in the Legion Bar in Three Lakes that Arthur was "henpecked," but that just shows how dumb we were. Sure, you loved to hear Charlie's stories and all the gossip this side of Eagle River, and Arthur would be sociable as a stone and just as accepting, but the longer I live, the more I sense that Arthur kept that little family together more than Charlie did. It was Arthur who understood the game and loved it and adjusted to it. It's like the shortstop telling the third basemen: *Reach what you can, but don't sweat the rest.* I can't thank Arthur anymore, so I thanked the mallards.

Looking For the Rabbit

*E*very time I go walking the woods with Marion Moran I get the same feeling I used to get back in parochial school when the Seven-Foot Nun would keep Charlie Kaiser and me after class to make sure we weren't falling too far behind our peer group in the pursuit of excellence.

"You have to respect her," Charlie would say of our dedicated teacher. "She knows more than God."

Her knowledge was awesome, and while a lot of it came from books, a lot of it didn't. It always amazed us that she knew so much about stuff that we figured she wasn't supposed to know about. She was supposed to know Latin, but she wasn't supposed to know how to hit Clarence Lopac's best pitches, which she did with a cowled, peekaboo stance that reminded you of Stan Musial.

It was particularly unnerving when Clarence was fanning the rest of us on the same pitches she was nailing.

"Whattaya gonna do," Clarence would shrug, "with someone who hits wearing a rosary?"

Marion Moran has that same aura as she hikes around the Wisconsin countryside. She is simply one of the best naturalists around. To walk with her is not only an education but a privilege.

We walked the woods the other day, and I kept thinking how much Charlie Kaiser would have loved it. Not to mention Steady Eddy, Hugh Percy, or James Gaius Watt.

Marion says she loves the winter woods because in the snow, "it's like reading an open book."

It is if you know the language. Otherwise the scratchings and trackings are just a melange of hieroglyphics, mysterious as a computer microchip on a Scrabble board.

Marion also loves to stop at certain scratchings and trackings, survey them in silence and then ask: "What happened here?"

Every time she asks that, it reminds me of Maxine Kumin's poem, "The Presence," and words tinkle in the frozen landscape like wind chimes:

Something went crabwise across the snow this morning.
Something went hard and slow over our hayfield.
It could have been a raccoon
lugging a knapsack.
It could have been a porcupine

carrying a tennis racket.
It could have been something
supple as a red fox
dragging the squawk and spatter
of a crippled woodcock.
Ten knuckles underground
those bones are seeds now
pure as baby teeth
lined up in the burrow.
I cross on snowshoes
cunningly woven from
the skin and sinews of
something else that went before.

After Marion stops you often enough and gets you to looking long enough before you answer, you find yourself viewing
the tableau in front of you the way a detective views a crime
scene. Then it becomes an addiction, like working crosswords
or equations. Then you find yourself praying for more snow
and longer winters.

The rabbit tracks are no longer random craziness, but an
unspooling record of night travels as accurate and complete as
a piece of film shot in infrared.

You see now the leisurely trail pace with no danger per-
ceived.

You see now the forty-five-degree cuts where the rabbit
fed on the sumac stems, the cuts as clean as blade-made.

You see now the rabbit of the past night, still present in
the daylight.

Knowledge has brought a whole new dimension to your
mind's eye. The scene is a hologram. And you are now seeing
around corners.

The next time Marion stops, the rabbit tracks and the
rabbit pellets take you only so far. You stand there in the snow,
not entirely dumb, just mute. Now, you do not understand what
is in front of you, let alone what is around the corner. *A rabbit
was here* . . . and *then* . . . and *then?*

Marion waits the way the Seven-Foot Nun always waited.
Did she know about holograms way back then? Was that why
she asked you if you got the picture, if you were *seeing* it?

Marion points out the delicate tracery, fanlike near a depression in the snow. You guess owl then. Wing marks. She says owl, tail mark. She doesn't think the wings ever touched. She says it's circumstantial. No blood. No fur. No struggle. It's as though the rabbit stepped into an elevator. And . . . left.

Trees rub and squeak in the wind. No other lives are moving.